AN ANGLO-AM[ERICAN]
TRAVELLER'S I[...]
1817

**A Yorkshire Quaker Merchant's Journey
by Sail, Steam and Sail**

© *Valda A. Swain*

First published November 1992

All rights reserved. No part of this book may be reproduced (except for normal review purposes) or utilised or stored in any way or by any means without the prior written consent of Autobus Review Publications Ltd.

ISBN 0 907834 28 0

Cover design by Alec Swain

Typeset by Autobus Studios

Printed by Bakes & Lord Ltd., Beacon Road, Bradford BD6 3NB

Autobus Review Publications Ltd., 42 Coniston Avenue, Queensbury, Bradford BD13 2JD. England.

FOREWORD

One of the ambitions of writers of 'a good read' is to induce in the reader a desire to turn the page and find out what happened next.

Writers of diaries succeed in doing this almost, it seems, without effort and although John Adamson clearly lived a life of diligence and hard work he managed to provide a wonderfully effortless read in this account of his trip to America nearly two hundred years ago.

I myself love diaries and I know that on my own shelves James Lees-Milne, Kilvert, Parson Woodforde, Thomas Turner and even the great Samuel Pepys himself are going to welcome the company of John Adamson.

Paul Eddington

Paul Eddington CBE
August 1992

INTRODUCTION

These diaries, four in number, were loaned to me by a cousin, Kenneth Adamson, great-great-great-grandson of the man who so graphically documents his 6 months' trip to and in America in 1817.

Every day, come storm, sea-sickness, intolerant heat or business dealings, he records what he sees, hears and experiences during his travels which took him from his home in Longroyd Bridge, Huddersfield, West Yorkshire by stage-coach to Liverpool, thence by Packet Ship across the Atlantic Ocean to Boston, on the east coast of America. Once there, he travels approximately 1500 miles by land and water, and all along his journey he comments on the way of life locally, describing the towns and villages he visited, talking of the slave trade and documenting the various Quaker meetings he attended.

The whole is a marvellous historical and social document of the time, and having read them I was immediately convinced that they should be published for others to enjoy rather than merely be returned to some dusty resting place. The content of the four diaries led to many months of extensive research for illustrations and other material before their publication was possible.

My involvement with the Adamson family comes via my mother's sister who married an Adamson, and I am deeply grateful to my cousins, the present custodians of the diaries, for their permission to publish. More recently, following the death of an old family member, numerous other extremely valuable papers, including portraits, came to light, some of which are included within these pages as, I hope, interesting background material.

Having spent a vast amount of time researching the 'Adamsons', and particularly John, I feel that I now really know him, and I am sure that he would be thrilled (and perhaps astonished) to know that you, a reader in the 1990s, were appreciating his writings. What a pity that in spite of the advance of science, and the ability to send men to the moon and beyond, we cannot travel back in time to meet him !

Valda A. Swain

Idle, Bradford

September 1992

PUBLISHER'S NOTE

Very little punctuation appears in the four diaries, although enough has been inserted to make meanings clearer. Except for this, the text is exactly as it appears in the hand-written originals. It will also be observed that many of the spellings are not as those customarily used today. These too have been retained in the following pages exactly as John Adamson wrote them. Similarly, all the drawings contained within the diaries have been reproduced alongside the appropriate text, all of which was written in ink.

BACKGROUND TO JOHN ADAMSON

John Adamson was born on the 14th March 1784, one of six children of William Adamson and his wife Rebekah. His ancestors had been Quakers from the very early 1700s and the family is well documented in Quaker records. His father was a husbandman and his grandfather a weaver. John Adamson was the fourth child of the family, which comprised four boys and two girls. His mother died when he was but five years old, after which his father ultimately remarried. This second marriage produced three boys, all of whom are documented in Quaker records, although it is understood that his father's second wife was not herself a Quaker. John, together with some of his brothers and his sister Rebecca, attended Ackworth School, a fine Quaker seat of learning near Pontefract, West Yorkshire. References in the Quaker Monthly Meeting records indicate that the Adamson children were financially assisted at the school.

In June 1809 John Adamson married Mary Beaumont, daughter of Joseph and Mary Beaumont of Pennistone, West Yorkshire. Joseph was a clothier, as was John at the time of his marriage, when he was shown as living at Wooldale, near Huddersfield. John's wife Mary was also a prominent Quaker. A copy of John's birth certificate and a 'condensed' family tree is included elsewhere within these pages.

In the diaries there is evidence that John's travelling companion on his journey to America was a merchant by the name of John Fisher of Spring Vale, Huddersfield whose wife Phoebe

This present-day view shows Ackworth School, a fine Quaker seat of learning where John Adamson received his education. (F.G.Davies)

was also involved with the Quaker movement. It would appear that it was John Fisher who was in charge of the trip and that John Adamson was responsible for all the letter writing and clerical activities etc.

There were four children to John Adamson's marriage, some of whom also attended Ackworth School as will be deduced from the letter shown later written by one of his sons whilst at Ackworth to his father. It would appear however that the Quaker involvement ended with John's children.

At the time of his journey to America, John Adamson lived at Longroyd Bridge, near Huddersfield, although it has not proved possible in more recent times to locate either his house or its site. This indicates that it may possibly no longer exist, having like so many old properties been swallowed up into some new development during the twentieth century. At a later date, John apparently set up his own company which is listed in old Trade Directories as 'John Adamson and Son, Wool Staplers, Green Dragon Yard, Huddersfield' and also at Bridge Street, Bradford. At the time of the 1851 Census, John Adamson had moved to Bradford and was living at 59 High Street (now part of Barkerend Road close to the city centre) with his wife and sons Edward and John, and two servants. John's daughter Emma married a Mr. Smith and died in childbirth at the age of 23. Very little is known of his other son, William.

Exterior and interior views of the Quaker Meeting House at Wooldale in West Yorkshire as it looks today. The Meeting House was licenced as a place of worship on 10 October 1689 following the Act of Toleration. (Courtesy of Wooldale Quakers)

John Adamson died on the 13th August 1857, his address at that time still being 59 High Street, Bradford, and he was buried in the Quaker section of Undercliffe Cemetry, Bradford, West Yorkshire, close to where his wife Mary lays.

DIARY ONE

Left home for Liverpool 3rd month 21st my wife accompanying me to that place. The wind not being in our favour I assisted J.F. to do business till 5th day evening the 27th our wifes with two of J.F.'s daughters left us the same day for home. We accordingly went on board the Liverpool Packet with our luggage and three other passengers. In the morning of the 28th the wind being unfavourable and the pilot not thinking it prudent to put out to sea the passengers were allowed to go ashore, the Captain accompanying us in a boat which was pleasing to us all I believe as the weather appeared dark and rough. I attended on J.F. doing some little business awaiting for the wind to come round to our favour which was not until the 3rd day and first of the 4th month, which had given us time to hear from our families after their reaching home, being all well and comfortable which was very satisfactory to us. The wind now being what seamen call fair the Captain and passengers went off to the ship in a small boat which was then under way and waiting for us in the River Mersey the pilot being anxious to be going. One of our passengers not being ready to embark with us in the boat caused us to have to wait nearly a full hour, the captain and pilot got almost out of patience till at last he arrived in the boat after which we set sail for Boston and got out of the Mersey as far as Ormeshead lighthouse. Being a fine and pleasant day our pilot left us here and we wrote to our families by him to put into the post office.

4th day the 2nd

Sailed off Holyhead in the evening the moon rising clean appeared most beautiful indeed. In the morning part of this day I became very sick and threw up a lot of bile after which I got much better. J.F. and myself got some water gruel made which was very nourishing. So went to bed.

This cabin of a Packet Ship exhibited at Falmouth Maritime Museum shows the type of accommodation which would have been used by John Adamson on his trans-Atlantic voyage in 1817. Of meagre size when compared with present-day cabins it nevertheless included a wardrobe, bed, locker and mirror, and as can be seen was equipped with a bowl and water jug for washing purposes. (Lt.Cdr J.W.Beck R.N. - Falmouth Maritime Museum)

5th day the 3rd

The morning rose bright with the wind in our favour having all sail spread we scudded before the wind nicely. At 12 o'clock the Captain and Mate took an observation, although I am not an entire stranger to these calculations yet it is very curious to look through the Quadrant at 12 o'clock. The sun appears crimson red just at the horizon of the water. Today we saw many ships all round about us sailing for different parts which was very pleasant it looking like a little company for us. This day ended with clear evening and pleasant weather.

6th day the 4th

This morning was very light with a fine breeze from south east and our ship sailing at the rate of 6 knots an hour and in the Atlantic Ocean quite clear of Ireland the sailors now cleared all cumbustables off the deck and made ready for sailing along. The men are particularly civil to each other and if the Captain or Mate gives any order all the men on deck who are on duty instantly proceed to the spot speaking the word and repeating what is ordered, that the Captain or Mate may understand that they know what he says. At 12 o'clock the Captain and Mates took an observation the ship sailing at about 8 knots an hour. The water here is of a beautiful light blue and clear as glass. Our ships company consists in all 26 persons. The Captain and first and 2nd Mate, 5 cabin passengers 3 steerage -do- 12 seamen the cook who is a Black man the Steward of the ship who has the stores under his call and a cabin boy. we had also on board 6 pigs 2 live sheep besides several dozens of ducks and fowls - so for meat and drink plenty. The first and 2nd Mate get there meals in the cabin along with the Captain and passengers. The duty of the first mate appears to be pretty much with the Captain giving orders to the sailors about the steering of the vessel as also taking an a/c of goods shipped and unshipped - taking observations of latitude etc. That of the 2nd mate seems to be that of ordering the seamen when out of employ in making ropes and having all the tackling of the ship as well as properly stowing everything into its propper place and to keep a look out when the Captain and first Mate are in bed or at their meals at which time the men obey his commands the same as the Captain and with the greatest despatch and civility. The seamen on our ship lived very well indeed having change of diet almost every day, such as Pudden one day, Pork and beans and peas the next, Beef and potatoes another and so on with anything that was taken off the Captains table. There manner of taking there meals is very plain for instance if it is the Beef and Potatoes it is all put in to a Kit that may hold about 4 or 5 gallons the meat and potatoes are all put in together and if a fine day the men sit down around it on the deck taking each man his knife out of his pocket then helps himself to a biscuit with some beef and potatoe after which each man has about a gill of rum served out which they mix with water to their own liking. They have generally about 3 meals a day, coffee and biscuits to breakfast, Pudden or meat for dinner and also supper. In the evening preceding this day we observed the sea along the sides of the ship to sparkle like sparks of fire the Captain informed us it was a sign of a southerly wind which accordingly came to pass most of this day, and wind blowing from the south and a good day for sailing as the ship got nearly 120 miles. Towards the evening we had nearly a calm which is unpleasant as the ship rolls about more than in steady sailing.

7th day morning the 5th

Still morning with smooth sea the ship making from 2 to 3 Knots. 12 o'clock overcast and cloudy yet a breeze springing up from north east we got on pretty well at about 5 Knots an hour. The manner in which they tell how fast the ship sails is by a small cord wound round a reel which they fasten to a board about the size of a truncheon and every two hours they throw it into the sea a man holding the reel and another holding a sand glass that is calculated to run through in a certain number of seconds. When the sand is through the man that holds the glass calls out stop which is instantly done after which the knots upon the cord are counted and the memorandum made, a knot is computed at about a mile. The main mast of our ship was from the deck to the top of the highest sail 110 ft the extremity of the yard-arms of same is about 90 feet wide which the main sail is fastened to and when the sail is spread it appears of an astonishing height and bredth. The day closed comfortably with a light breeze from the eastward.

1st day morning the 6th

A fine pleasant morning with a little wind from the south east, the passengers kept the order of the day by clean washing shaving changing etc. as becomes everyone and one of our friends at breakfast remarked that he hoped we knew what day it was and endeavoured to make propper use of it to which I believe the rest joined in Amen. The sailors also wash and shave keeping good order among themselves in the forecastle of the ship which is there room both to sit and sleep in when not on duty on the deck. Although we had not the opportunity of seeing people going to their respective places of worship nor of hearing the sound of bells round about the neighbourhood yet there appeared something of a Sabbath Day. I felt pleased at the crowing of the cocks on board it seemed very domestick especially the duck and cat who were quite at home and in good liking. About noon this day I observed some of the sailors reading there

Testament and others who I supposed could not read were set by and dilegently attending to what the others were reading. One of them read aloud in the Epistle of Paul when he was cast onto the Island of Malta, so the day closed a fine mild night.

2nd day the 7th

A particularly fine morning the wind from south east. About 8 o'clock the Mate got the men to work in making ropes which is a certain sign of steady sailing. To one not tired of the sea it is pleasant to observe the ship in full sail and the men busy at their ropemaking turning away as comfortable as may be. About 11 o'clock a ship stood to the north of us but did not incline to speak. The order of our ship same as all others was divided into watches according to the number of hands sometimes every two and other times every 4 hours it generally begins at 12 o'clock at noon when the altitude of the sun is is taken which is done by one of the men ringing a bell extended over the forecastle of the ship. The men coming on duty immediately begin to pump the little water made last watch, relieve at the helm and throw out the Tag Line to ascertain at how many knots an hour the ship is sailing with any alteration that may be necessary in sails rigging etc. in the evening a calm, the ship rolling about very unpleasantly.

3rd day the 8th

At 8 o'clock a smooth sea with a good deal of swell, I became very poorly and sick again. At 12 o'clock the Captain took an observation and the wind briskened from the north west and in the evening rain with appearance of bad weather.

4th day the 9th

After a rolling night the wind veered round to the eastward briskly with a good deal of sea, yet a good day for sailing the ship having gone at 12 o'clock at noon in the last 24 hours 140 miles. This evening our sailors killed one of the pigs which they were very dextrous about. To make the salt water take effect in scalding, when hot they pound about the size of a mans fist of rosin and sprinkle it over the pig previous to pouring the water on which bring the hare off very clean indeed. They then extend it in some part about the vessel after which they open it take out the Intrells and heave them overboard into the sea and the slaughter is completed. This evening closed mild with pleasant weather.

5th day the 10th

Grey morning wind south east. About 8 o'clock a whale passed alongside of us and in the afternoon we saw some large black fish rolling along like black pigs (the Porpoises) in the water. It is a rule in all ships to keep what seamen call a Log Book. Our ships book was rough cartridge paper with a sail cloth back and kept by the first mate his name James Morgan. It is headed and ruled with collums for the purpose and almost every transaction of the day is noted down in this book on every watch wether 2 or 4 hours what has passed on board is then memorandum'd in the Log Book such as what Knots the ship has gone at what way the wind hath blown, how the ship hath been steered what alteration hath taken place in the sails ropes etc. also what has been for dinner and at the close of every day which is reckoned at 12 o'clock at noon when the altitude of the sun is to be ascertained the mate gives his general remarks in the Log Book as above how the last 24 hours hath passed. The Captain keeps another private book called the Seaman's Journal which he makes his calculations in also copying some of the Log Book such parts as he thinks propper. This book he keeps pretty much to himself not liking any of the passengers or others to overlook him while he keeps it. I recollect one of our company asking very civilly to look into it but the Captain refused saying he would rather he foreswear opening it though the person had it in his hand at the same time. The Log Book is not so private as the passengers are at times allowed to amuse themselves with it. This day closed with a mild evening and pretty comfortable night.

6th day the 11th

A still fine morning with a little wind. About 11 o'clock a ship appeared in sight ahead of us and in a short time she appeared inclined to speak which civility was returned by our ship. The minuver of the two ships to a stranger was both curious and interesting. She proved to be the Cape Packet an English ship from the Cape Of Good Hope bound for London had been out at sea 50 days. An oldish ship and rather leaky J.F. and myself with the others of our company got each of us a letter on board of her to our families and friends which was a great gratification. As the manner of ships speaking to each other at sea may amuse someone at a future day not accustomed to such scenes I will note down here so near as I can recollect the circumstances of the above. When the ship appeared ahead of us it was known throughout that of ours in a short time. The Captain called the boy to bring the jack he looking through his glass at her for some time, he pronounced her an English ship which we soon all found out by her colours. He percieved she inclined to speak and ordered our colours hoisting which were American viz, a blue flag with 13 white stars on it denoting the 13 Unites States of America. Both watches of our sailors were ordered on deck to stand to their positions in backing the sails in which duty they showed themselves to advantage. When the two ships had minuvered round to their propper distance our Captain stood on the 1/4 deck and ours being the larger ship he put the speaking trumpet to his mouth and hailed out who are you, to which the Captain from the Cape answered by his trumpet the Cape Packet from the Cape of Good Hope bound for England to London 50 days out, who are you? to which our captain answered the Liverpool Packet from Liverpool bound to Boston been at sea 10 days Longitude 25. Will you let us put a few letters on board of you to which the Cape captain answered in the sea phrase Aye Aye bring us some newspapers. Our Captain replied Aye Aye and ordered the boat to be let down into the sea with 3 or 4 men who rowed to the ship and gave the letters and newspapers to the Cape Captain and returned. Our people drew up the boat to the stern of the ship after which both ships took there own courses and the business ended - all which had certainly been very pleasant to us. A speaking trumpet is about 2 feet in length but much wider than any other instrument of the trumpet kind. It has also an oval top convenient for a persons lips to move in and a person knowing how to speak through it properly can speak very loud indeed. In the evening a south west wind with appearance of bad weather.

7th day the 12th

A rainy wild morning the wind strong from south west and in the evening blew strong from the west with rolling sea.

1st day the 13th

A wild morning with a frightful sea and continued until evening.

2nd day the 14th

A strong westerly wind the ship pitching rather violent with no appearance of a change and several of the passengers complained of being unwell myself one but by taking a little oatmeal gruel I soon recovered. I in strong terms recommend the use of water and oatmeal made into a gruel as I found it at sea the most nourishing as well as the greatest preventative against the sickness of anything yet prescribed. Some of the passengers recoursed to wine and brandy but one of them became at last glad to take gruel 3 times a day and another lay in bed and on the sofa pretty much who did not take gruel so that nothing of the store kind which we had brought for our voyage was equal to our canister of oatmeal.

3rd day the 15th

Wild and rough the wind strong from south east and the sea rolling awfully. Our ship was now almost stripped of her sails. The yardarms of the Gallants were taken down in short everything not necessary in a gale in the rigging and on deck was stowed down into the room underneath and such as was not portable enough to put away was tied down fast to prevent them from rolling up and down the deck. The man at the helm even put off his shoes the motion of the ship became so quick, and at meal time the egs and knifes pots etc. were almost constantly tumbling onto the floor with tea or whatever might be in them. The sea now broke over the deck very frequently. I believe most of the passengers got wet was they ever so cautious. I took great care indeed. I stood in the cabin stairs. The top was drawn over and one of the doors shut but after all a wave broke over the side of the vessel and rushed in at the half door which completely immersed me in salt water. The passengers on the outside were nearly up to the boot tops in spray. No appearance of a change in the evening.

4th day the 16th

Still rolling and pitching dreadfully. Towards evening the wind and sea moderated a little which was by us all I believe received as a favour from him who can still both wind and wave.

5th day morning the 17th

Fine with smooth sea with a little swell and gentle south east wind, the sailors once again hoisted up the arms and sails which was a pleasing sight. We had this morning the pleasure of seeing a Man of War bird from Newfoundland a token that its native country was not at any great distance. We now almost daily see whales spouting and porpoise fish playing alongside the ship. In the evening a thick fog and starlight night.

6th day the 18th

Fine sun shining morning with a fresh breeze from south east which continued until evening. A good day for sailing. In the night a calm and wind changed to north.

7th day the 19th

Wet cold morning the wind from north east. It now came on rain and sleet very bad for sailors all being so slippery cold and wet. Just at the edge of the banks of Newfoundland we saw 3 or 4 ships sailing different directions as also great flock of sea fowl of diverse kinds. Our sails being wet and held the wind which took us along about 9 knots an hour. Today I observed the men to have each his work bag with thread thimble needles etc. When not on duty they mend their cloths at which work they are very handy in their way. We brought on board a half chest of oranges which today we opened and found a great part of them in a state of decay a proof of their being a fruit difficult to preserve good at sea. At 2 o'clock today the air was so cold that the ropes sails and the mens cloths were frose over as on a 1st months day at Huddersfield. The wind continued to blow fresh until evening a good day for sailing yet extremely cold. I enjoyed a comfortable nights sleep.

1st day morning the 20th

Clear smooth sea and very sharp weather. The thermometer now stood at 33 which on the 16 stood at 60 a proof of the severity of weather on the banks of Newfoundland which we now experienced. Our chief Mate discovered the ice at a distance and in a short time myself with the rest of our company saw it very fair from of the Quarter Deck. Three seperate islands of great magnatude floated above water almost as high as our ships masts. These are awfull companions to ships at sea and very much dreaded by seamen. Our ship bore away from them as much as possible so as to avoid striking. The wind now at north west blew us from these dreadful objects. At 4 o'clock in the afternoon we again fell in with the ice. Two large islands one appeared to be as large as a 2 acre field and a train of lumps extending for 1/2 a mile in length. Our ship had to twist first one way then another to avoid them. The weather was particularly fine and the sea smooth all which was greatly in our favour as such obstackles are extremely dangerous in rough weather and in the dark. Along the bank we were accompanied by a swarm of sea fowl as thick as rooks in a rookery. The sea here abounds with excellent Codfish on a sandy bottom. Over where we sailed we found it to be about 42 fathoms. Our men threw out the hook and line but the vessel was going rather too quick to give the fish an opportunity to bite and our being so near the ice the Captain did not chuse to stop her on such a trifling a pastime. The water hear appears much like clean river water. the ice mountains are as white as firm lump sugar, standing out of the sea a prodigious height. In the evening a calm which lasted until 4 o'clock in the morning of

2nd day the 21st

which was very acceptable as both the ship and the ice remained stationary till the daylight appeared to give us light to steer ourselves clear. The wind at daybreak arose from east exact as we could wish for so the Father of Mercies protects his undeserving children in their peril and distress. Now we got over the banks yet the air still blew cold over the Ice Mountains. At 11 o'clock we were favoured with a fine easterly breeze - our ship sailed at about 8 Knots an hour in her direct course. At 4 o'clock it got to a gale with rain and a mountainious sea. In the evening the gale became so violent the Captain was obliged to bring the ship to the wind, what seamen call laying to. In the night came on lightening.

3rd day the 22nd

The wind moderated but the sea rolled in mountains we were not able to sail until the evening when both the wind and sea became more settled. Our sailors killed one of the sheep today and very nice it was to have been at sea 3 weeks with only a little hog.

4th day the 23rd

Wild and rough the wind north - the sea continued to break frequently over the deck drenching everything in its way with salt water. in the evening heavy rain with lightening and thunder.

5th day the 24th

The wind continued blowing a gale, the ship laying to until towards the evening, a little interval or moderation which lasted most of the night

6th day the 25th

The gale this morning resumed its usual violence the wind from south and very warm. The thermometer which a few days back stood at 33 now rose to 65 and accompanied with heavy rain. The first mate expressed in my hearing that he did not recollect the wind ever being higher than during some part of this storm. We made but little progress in sailing for most part of a week the wind being contrary and the ship laying to during the whole time. The ships crew and passengers were favoured with pretty good health except the Captain who was attacked with a bowel complaint.

7th day the 26th

This morning the gale somewhat abated but the wind continued contrary. The atmosphere cleared with a cooling breeze yet not favourable to our course. The evening commenced with beautiful moonlight which lasted until daybreak.

1st day the 27th

This morning arose most charmingly bright, a gentle breeze from north east in our favour. The thermometer stood in the shade at 54. Our sailors now begun to hoist up the yard arms and to open once again the Gallants, Royal and Studding sails which had to be laid to one side for near a whole week. We had also in sight three vessesls making the same course as ourselves which was very pleasant. The sea was now becoming as calm as a fish pond so the great master of the universe orders the elements for his own all wise purposes which if man would give time for reflection he would no doubt see and find things which at first felt across to the inclination to afterwards turn out to advantage and a blessing. Our water now smelt very bad but the taste was not so disagreeable. The Captain observed that the ship had now consumed 12 hundred gallons of fresh water more than had been gone through in the same length of time on any former passage. At 1/2 past five o'clock we came up with one of the vessels which we had seen in the morning. Our Captain spake her, it proved to be a large brig called the Richards come from Bristol and bound for Philadelphia had been at sea 22 days. the same cerimony was pretty much made use of as when we spake the Cape Packet on the 11 inst. The brig appeared to have many people on board amongst which were wimmen and children. I was pleased to see a woman with a child in her arms sat on deck as comfortable to all appearances as if on land. The two captains asked each other if they was in need of anything and was very civil. In the evening a fine breeze from the south which continued all night.

2nd day the 28th

Mild morning with a southerly wind and the sea rather high. The thermometer stood in the shade on the deck at 65 and in the cabin at 63. Towards noon the wind got high with heavy rain and rough sea. At 4 o'clock the wind changed northward and the thermometer 50 in the shade on the deck. Our sailors today killed our 2nd and last sheep. This day closed wet and foggy.

3rd day the 29th

Bright morning and smooth sea the wind north the thermometer stood in the cabin at 50 and in the shade on the deck at 47. A fair wind and good sailing all day and continued so much of the night.

4th day the 30th

Fair north wind and a pleasant morning, the ship going at 8 knots thermometer in the cabin at 51 and on deck in the shade at 40. The weeds now began to float alongside of us and the water became more like the colour of river water, a certain proof that we approached nearer to the shores. At 10 o'clock we spoke the ship Milton from Boston had sailed on first day morning the 27th bound for Amsterdam. The Captain of above ship gave our Captain information that his family was well also that an old woman of his aquaintance was deceased. Our sailors today got out cables and fixed them to the anchors. The day closed calm.

5th day. 1st of 5th month

Shining morning with calm sea, the thermometer stood in the shade on deck at 40 and in the cabin at 51. At 12 o'clock the mate sounded and found a sandy pebble bottom in 55 fathoms of water. The Captain ordered a hook and line throwing out. He in a short time had a large plump cod fish on deck which we had dressed for dinner. It was excellent being so fresh and a change. At 12 o'clock the sea became quite calm that the vessel stood nearly still. The fish hook and line was again let down when JF and myself shortly drew up a very large cod fish. I supposed it to weigh 40lbs. which would have sold in Huddersfield for 13/-. One of the men again let the line down and caught two more in about 10 minutes. If the vessel had been anchored according to the Captains account we could very soon have taken 1000 as cod and diverse other fish abound here such as haddock, allabot crab soles etc. We were now come upon Georges Bank about 200 miles from Boston. A mild calm evening and still night.

6th day 5th month 2nd

Fine spring morning with calm sea. Our men now began to clean and varnish the vessel and to make all tidy for sailing into port. Both Captain and men seemed to pride themselves in having all particularly nice which has a pleasing appearance both in ships as well as houses. the weather was greatly in there favour being settled and fine. Today we saw several ships the sea smooth and the evening mild with a still night.

7th day 5th month 3rd

We now begin to look out for land with fine weather and wind in our favour. The passengers got to washing and dressing in readyness to go on shore which was a pleasing prospect having not seen land for full 4 weeks. At 11 o'clock we discovered the desired object the American shores extending along our left. Our signal was now hoisted it was a ball painted red and fastened to the top of the main mast. About 6 o'clock the flag for the pilot was hoisted and we soon observed him coming towards us. He got onto the deck of our ship 40 minutes after 7 o'clock. the Captain gave up command of the vessel immediately and all the men attended to the pilot's order very strictly with the activity usual on ships going into port. Boston habour is very formidable it has 52 islands about its entrance and most of them forts mounted with cannon. the wind blew a gentle breeze in our favour so at 9 o'clock we passed the castle at the mouth of the habour just as the soldiers sounded 9 o'clock and by 10 o'clock our ship was safely moored at anchor. The Captain and 3 of our passengers went on shore. the letterbags were sent to the post office at same time, so after a passage of 32 days we safely arrived on the American shore and I trust our minds were exercised with thankfullness to the great preserver of negligent and forgetful man.

This sketch shows a typical street in Bradford, England during the early nineteenth century.

DIARY TWO

1st day 5th month 4th

Being so late when the ship anchored J.F. and myself thought it best to sleep on board to fear of getting into damp beds on the shore in a strange place, so by the time we had dressed and got breakfast on first day morning the men had got the ship close to the pearhead that we had only to stride of the deck of the ship onto dry land which we accordingly did and walked into the town of Boston for the first time the place where our friends suffered so much persecution for our religeous principals. Here is in this town a friends meeting house and grave yard which is now shut up. It is taken care of by the master of the Exchange Coffee House, who dries a few cloths in it. We took up our lodging at the coffee house above named. It is a large convenient house where people of different nations resort to for accomodations being similar to the houses at the Bathing Places in England.

2nd day the 5th

Wrote home by way of New York a ship being about to sail to England from thence.

3rd day the 6th and 4th day the 7th

Wrote to John Beaumont, John Hustler, Joseph Haigh and to my wife all which letters I put into the office of Winslow Lewis & Co. owners of the Brig Falcon which was ready to sail for Liverpool. On **5th day the 8th** J.F wrote home this day by the same vessel.

6th day the 9th

I wrote home to my wife again from Boston by the ship Tritan going to Liverpool. In the evening I went up to the top of the Exchange on the outside of which is an observatory from whence may be seen the whole town as also the bay. The new and principal houses are built of brick but a great many more are built entirely from wood and in a very neat form. The doors windows shutters and the houses themselves are painted and washed with a drab colour which gives them a neat appearance to a stranger accustomed to smoky buildings. the fires are generally wood even the respectable houses. Their fireplaces generally consist of a bare open hearth with two iron bars something like an English grid iron with 4 feet: they stand on the hearth about 4 or 6 inches high. The fire side of these irons are in good rooms pollished a little and some have brass fronts made bright. On these they lay their wood across and light it which soon makes blaze. There are a many poor people here who appear to make it their sole business to saw wood from house to house with a small saw about a yard long and 2 or 3 inches broad strung in a frame much like a bow and arrow. With this strong saw they can cut up a large lump of firewood in a short time. Boston is nearly surrounded with a bay and wonderfully adapted by nature to keep out an enemy. The entrance is about a 1/4 mile wide and on each side are islands upon which forts are built and mounted with cannon. Here are in this bay 52 of these small islands which stand high out of the water so that the cannon mounted on these little hills have great command on the bay and would be able to destroy a great deal of ships in a short time. This town and bay is the most fortyfied of any in the United States.The ships of war lay in here. they have a government naval dock where they repair and build the state vessels. Boston is supposed to contain about 35,000 inhabitants. In the publick streets they appear clean and well dressed. There manners seem a little different to England. They appear to rise sooner in a morning: the genteel people will be all alive and stiring about business soon after six o'clock in a morning and by a little after nine in the evening the shops are shut up and the streets are quite still from the hurry of business. From what I have observed people in general are more moderate in their way of living - great Inns are not so common as in England. Lodging houses are the places for the accommodation of travellers and strangers, respectable houses of this description charge about 2 dollars a day for lodgings and board. They are very regular in their mealtimes. At the Exchange Coffee House where J.F. and myself lodged in the town of Boston they had breakfast at 8 dinner at 2 tea at 6 and supper at 9 o'clock a bell being rung and the table set out very punctually. The travellers or others at the house almost immediately repared to the dining room where the master of the house was set at the head of the table ready to assist the waiting in carving etc. for his company which would consist sometimes of 40 or 50 persons. Every person is helped to what he chuses on the table and water in one decanter and brandy in another for beverage which some take to the clean water and others mix a little brandy with it. Neither Ale nor Porter ever appeared on the table to my knowledge. When a person has taken what he likes he rises from his chair, not waiting any cerimony: if he has only sat 5 minutes it seems to make no difference in that case. At the publick tables of this kind people do not stop after meals all together to drink wine, this practice seems not to be known or at least practiced in the town except while people are taking their meal. If they wish to have wine it is furnished with a label put upon the neck of the bottle, it is brought to table in the common bottle, not poured into the English white glass decanter so the person calling for it takes what he chuses and the remainder of it is set by until he calls for it at the next meal. Here are a great many black people in Boston especially amongst the labouring classes. A labouring person can earn about 2 dollars a day that is about equal to 9/- sterling and provisions are cheaper than in England. Shambles meat sells on an average at about 5d/per lb. sterling or American Federal about 9 or 10 cents so that poor people have an opportunity of living more comfortably than in England. Fire wood is also low as almost anyone who has heard of America has heard how plentiful wood is. Flower sells much in proportion as in England, freight etc. considered, because where it is allowed to be shipped to our country the price regulates itself accordingly. Here are also in the bay or rather over it about 6 wood bridges they are built upon wooden pillors on posts drove down in the bottom of the water some of them appear to be a 1/4 others 1/2 and some nearly 3/4 of a mile in length. They are strong and convenient. Large trees are also suffered to grow in the town more than England. A person standing on the outside of a roof may almost fancy the place to be in a wood. Flat roofs are common, on which people sit and walk dry their cloths air their beding etc. I have not hitherto observed any person intoxicated in the streets a practice that disgraces the English nation in the eyes of foreigners.

7th day the 10th

I attended with J.F doing business.

1st day the 11th

Being no meeting of friends here I kept my room pretty much and read in my bible, a small edition which I brought from home with me.

2nd day the 12th

Attended on J.F. doing business and writing. Today I shipped our boxes and luggage on board the sloop May for New York. Early this morning sailed for Liverpool the ship Triton, John Kilner of Huddersfield went passenger in her, who took a parcel for J.F.'s family. We also sent letters for home. In the bay by the above vessel in the evening being cool and pleasant I took a walk round the genteel part of the town and some most elegant houses there are, especially towards the end of the bay called the Liverpool Wharf.

3rd day the 13th

Packed up our linen etc. and prepared for our journey towards New Bedford.

4th day the 14th

Wrote for J.F. and also a letter home to Benjm Sebohm with a note enclosed for my wife desiring her to inform J.M. that I had attended to the earrond he gave me in charge of George Milnes. American carriages or publick coaches are not so elligant as in England. They are not known by the name of coach: they are all called stages built long but with little spring and from about 1/2 a yard from the bottom they are only oil cloth so that in hot weather they can roll it up and the stage becomes quite open; except overhead is a thin boarded cover without lining. In England we should call them small caravans as they are nothing more than this; no passengers or parcels ride on top; the driver sits low on a narrow seat before the same as the English covered carts; their horses are nimble and light and will take one of these stages 60 miles in 12 hours. They are seated before and behind with a form in the middle so when full they have three rows of people in the inside. The luggage is not put into a boot but is lashed or tied on a trellis frame behind, a most dangerous plan being very liable to shake off if not well secured.

5th day the 15th

At 4 o'clock this morning J.F. and myself left Boston in one of these stages that carried the mail, and on our way to New Bedford which place we reached about 4 o'clock in the afternoon after a pleasant ride and a fine day. The country from Boston to New Bedford is pretty level yet barren and rocky; it has all the appearance of once being an entire wood, the soil in general is stoney and bad, a little Indian corn with a mixture of Rye seems to be the principal corn grown in this part of America. The farm houses appear to have most of them large orchards of fruit trees from which their regular apple cyder beverage is manufactured. the prospect for most part of the road from Boston to New Bedford is wood with every few miles a lotment cleared of the wood and cultivated; then wood again a few miles and so on all the way a distance of 60 miles. We passed through the following villages in todays travel viz Sharon Taunton Middleborough and part of Fairhaven. the last is a short distance from New Bedford. Our stage driver had frequently to stop at the post offices; they were not in market towns as in England, but most generally a little and perhaps nearly a lone wood house and managed by some of the family of the adjoining farmer, so the letters are conveyed through the thin inhabited states. In our driving along the road today we observed a great many of the American burying grounds, several of which were close to the side of the road in the edge of the wood unenclosed on a dry little hill amongst the brushwood - some of them perhaps one might suppose a few families had been interred in and others more, with here and there a stragling grave stone set on end at the feet or head of the grave with a little inscription, others without any stone and some had a rough common stone set up at the end of the grave that had never been dressed at all, only just taken loose from the next stone heap and laid at the head or feet of the deceased by some friend or relation and so left sacred to their memory. As well as I can recollect we passed between 12 to 15 of these burying places in two or three instances I noticed not more than from 6 to 12 or 14 graves. the driver informed me these were family burying grounds, none but relations of a family and yet these were unenclosed; a stranger would not be able to discover what they were but for the little blue tomb or grave stone being set up here and there with a short inscription to the memory of the deceased. We also passed many extensive ponds or lakes some appeared to cover nearly 400 acres of extent; fine clear water they are still called by the Indian names; as near to these waters formally used to be the settlements of the indians and I have been informed that it was with great reluctance they gave up these situations to the English; they were so convenient to them both for fresh water and for fish as also the wild animals of the woods resorting to these places to drink and cool themselves. I understand before they relinquished them they stood several conflicts with the new settlers but they are now a great while ago deserted by their first owners. J.F. and myself both thought we had not seen a house built of brick or stone in all the days ride a distance of 60 miles and near to New Bedford we actually observed some people removing a wood house we thought large enough to accommodate two families comfortably; they had blocks and oxen with rollers underneath they had shifted it more than 200 yards and where they were intending to go with it we did not see. The bridges in the country places are of a piece with other things in this thin inhabited part of the country. They consist if the brook be not very large of 3, 4 or 6 pieces of timber laid over the brook or creek and then laid across these timbers thick planks quite loose without a nail or pin to fasten them, so a bridge of a moderate size is soon constructed. Almost every house appears to have its well, the manner of drawing water is with wood pole as see drawing below, which acts as a weigh beam.

The houses in this part of the country as before observed are invariably made of wood as also the barns, cow houses, mills etc. Wood walls, wood roofs and wood eveything.

The drawing below shows the type of well common to most houses for the purpose of drawing water.

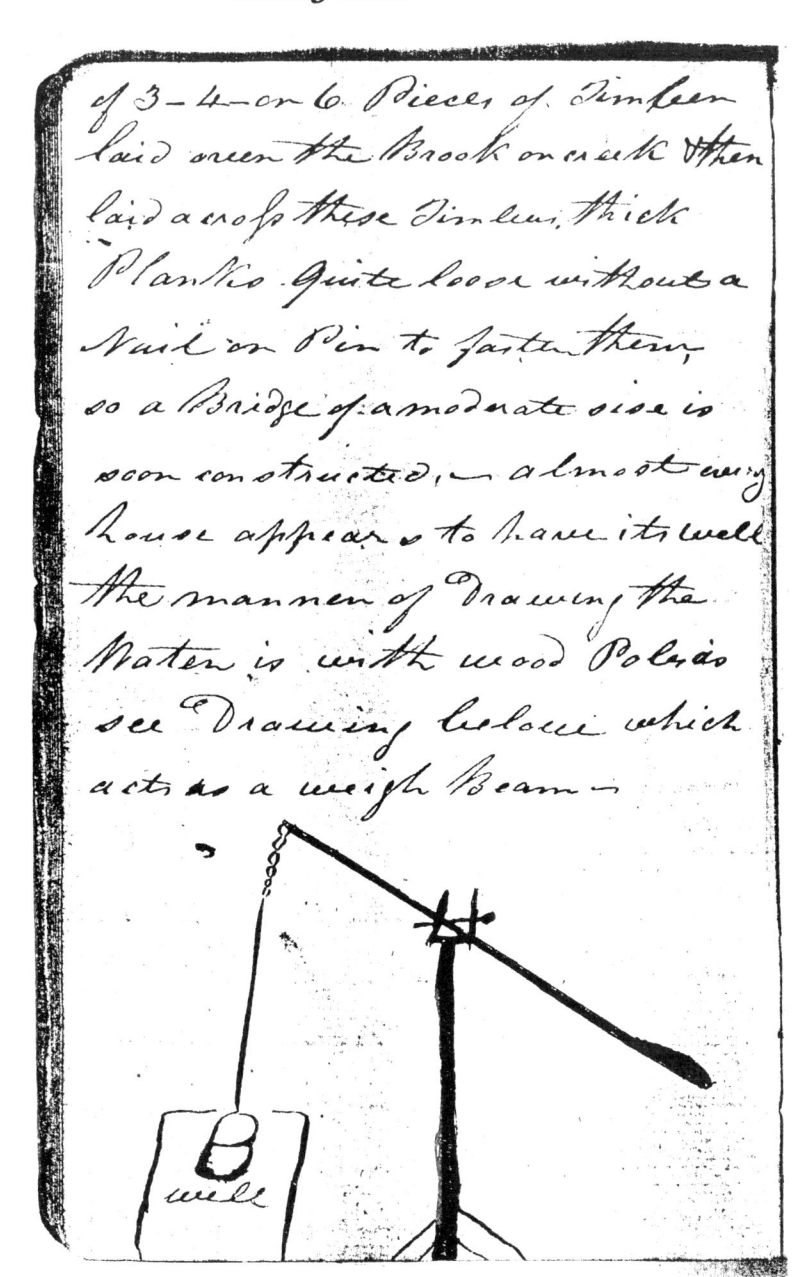

6th day the 16th

Being now at New Bedford myself and the luggage went to the Bedford Hotel kept by a person named Nelson a convenient roomy house and very clean comfortable beds. J.F. went to a friends house; a minister who had been in Europe on religeous service. He appeared to be quite an elderly person his name was William Rotch. Here are a many friends settled in this town. They appear to be of the principal and respectable classes. New Bedford is a clean pleasant small sea port, its inhabitants are computed at from about two thousand to 24 hundred. Here are, as in Boston a many coloured people resident at this place. The houses are all except two built of wood and generally very neatly painted, the main business of the townspeople is pretty much in the whale fishing trade. The labouring folks are employed in unloading and fitting out vessels for the above purpose, they go as far as Cape Horne and some of them are near two years in making a voyage. A friend's vessel arrived about 4 days ago at this wharf who has been out 20 months. She appeared to have a very good cargo of fish oil which I observed the ships crew unloading, they were most of them blacks. Herrings are also caught and cured at this port. They have a curious way of preparing them. when the boats bring them to shore they salt them: after which they run a small stick or rod about 3/4 of a yard long through the head of a number of fish and hang them up in a small square wood house made for that purpose; much as our English fancy waistcoat piecemakers hang their hanks of woollen weft up in the brimstone stove. They then kindle a fire of small chips underneath the fish and close the door upon them. They will keep the smook up for 2 or 3 days before the fish be sufficiently done so as to keep. I noticed also hams in this smook house preparing in the same way as the herrings, smooked ham is very common in America but its taste is so very different to the English ham that it is very disagreeable to most Yorkshiremen. Neat Packet sloops sail once or twice a week from hence - they will go from New Bedford to New York in about 24 hours if the wind is fair. they charge a person for passage etc. about 7 dollars or sterling 31/6d. Oxen are employed in this nation by the farmers generally; I have very rarely seen more than one horse in a draught or team employed in the farming branches. Their teams consist of 2 or 4 oxen without a horse. Some of the more respectable farmers will have their 4 oxen very large and near alike in size, colours and shape of their harness etc. which gives them a noble appearance and it is astonishing to see what an enormous load of wood or manure these 4 oxen will draw with ease and stability. At the Hotel of New Bedford they had a young woman servant who was an Indian and a real Native of the country, her name Lydia. She was of a darkish copper yellow colour and an active clean sharp girl. In the neighbourhood of this place as before observed, Indian tribes were settled, and there still remain several families who are become quite civilised and conform to the laws of the United States. I was informed by a respectable person at the Hotel aforesaid that such Indians were as good and intelligent citizens as any people could be - learning to read/write/keep accounts and become an usefull race of people as in any society possesing far superior abilities to the generallity of the Africans. A good cow may be bought at New Bedford from 35 to 40 dollars sterling £7.17s to £9. A good hansome 5 years old horse from 75 to 80 dollars sterling £16.17s to £18. cows and oxen are cheap but horses are dearer than in England. In this town there are different denominations of religious people; but none so numerous as the Society of Friends - they are a large gathering for so small a town. I conversed with one friend who informed me he thought the meeting consisted of more than two hundred members.

7th day the 17th

At 6 o'clock this morning we left New Bedford. Willm. Rotch sent his carriage and black servant Thomas with us as far as Jerimy Giffords at Bristol Ferry on our way to Providence from New Bedford to Howlands Ferry Bridge a distance of 20 miles. The country is much the same as from Boston to New Bedford; nearly over run with wood yet more barren and rocky - the cattle we observed from the road side were very poor, but on our approaching nearer the Howlands Ferry Bridge the prospect altered. We had a view of Rhode Island and the country more open and cleared of wood. Willm. Roche's servant set us down at Bristol Ferry where the Newport stage mail runs to. The bags and passengers are ferried over in a boat kept for the purpose and the stage from Bristol is waiting to take them forward to Bristol about 2 miles further, at which place it stops to dine. Bristol is a small sea port with about 2000 inhabitants. It has been a place that derived great proffits from the slave trade and yet carries it on under Spanish colours. Leaving here we proceeded forward to Providence passing through another small town called Warren it also laying to the sea shore. The land now began to appear more inland, the fields to look green and gardens pleasant as in England especially as we approached Providence which place we reached about 5 o'clock in the evening after a favourable journey of about 41 miles.

1st day the 18th

Being first day morning and now in Providence in the state of Rhode Island a place where a friends meeting is held J.F. and myself attended the morning meeting at 1/2 past ten; towards the close of which a woman friend addressed us in a few words advising friends to seek a city that hath foundations. People in Providence as well as other places in America are very punctual in attending their different places of worship and all appears particularly still on sabbath days. The town is built mostly upon the banks of a large river which is called by its own name Providence River: here is depth of water for vessels of 7 or 800 tons burthen to lay near the wharf. Over one part of the bay is built a large and commodious wood bridge which is a great improvement to the place. The houses are a mixture, some brick, some stone and others wood. They have here also a clean plan of washing or painting the outside light colour which has a pleasing appearance. The last account of the number of its inhabitants were 14 thousand. Here are several large cotton manufacturers carried on to advantage as also some woollen cloth concerns but the latter is at a stand, the peace with England put it out of there power to sell their goods but with considerable loss. This place took its name from the first settlers being obliged to shelter here when persicuted in the State of Massachsets for varying from the establishment in thier oppinion in matters of religion. It has much the appearance of an England town and to me appeared a very pleasant situation. At about 5 o'clock in the evening we took stage and left this place for New London passing through Planefield and Northwitch. The last is a village of considerable extent but being in the night we could not see the country so as to form a just idea of it; yet during the time it was daylight the land appeared barren and stoney. We passed several Indian houses near the woods which abound here, a passenger told us they had a meeting house and one or two of them owned large lotments of land.

2nd day the 19th

At 6 o'clock this morning we arrived at New London the place where the steam boat goes from to New York having travelled through the night from Providence to this place the distance of 59 miles. New London is a little clean looking town situate close to the side of the sound. Its business is farming and a little fishing. The English from the West Indies come here for cattle etc. This morning sailed out before us an English Brig and a Schooner both loaded with horses and cows for the West Indies about 2 weeks sail from hence. Our steam boat was 134 feet long and 34 feet wide the engine 50 horse power and fitted up in eligance to the astonishment of every stranger, having beds and other furniture of the very best kind, ample accomodation for 200 passengers; seperate appartments for women and everything convenient. The Captain whose name was Law who commanded the late misfortunate ship Jupiter informed us that the boat engine and all apperatus cost 8000 dollars or sterling £18000. We sailed along the shore and pretty quick she being flatish only drawing about 6 feet water but had the appearance of a Man of War being rigged with sails and marked for guns. We had a prospect of the State of Conneticut a mile to our right and Long Island on our left. She started from New London exact at 8 o'clock in the morning and we reached Newhaven a little before 5 having sailed the distance of about 50 miles. Here the steam boat from New York met us and exchanged passengers, luggage etc. The New York boat did not get up until near 7 o'clock as she had the longer rout by near 25 miles. During this time at leisure J.F. and myself walked about 1 1/2 miles from the beach up into the town of Newhaven. It is a beautiful situation on level and fertile ground, hansome houses and some elegant shops. the inhabitants are supposed to be about 5 thousand people - here is also a small wharf, vessels of two or three hundred tons burthen can lay to the pear. Fish is plentiful in the bay. The New York boat now being alongside of the New London one, we accordingly went on board - a friend was the Captain his name Saml. Bunker, a relation to Captain Bunker a friend we left at Liverpool commander of the ship Belfast laying for frieght in that port. As we had been up all the first day night travelling we went pretty soon to bed and about 4 o'clock next morning the Captain called out friend Fisher we are just entering the narrows. We directly got up and went on deck. New York very soon appeared and about 5 o'clock we got safe to the wharf having come from Newhaven to this place 80 miles by water in about 9 hours sooner that is usual by steam boats.

3rd day the 20th

Being arrived at New York we set about getting a lodging room and our luggage removed from the steam boat. The sloop also with our large boxes was arrived from Boston which was very acceptable to us as they contain our clean cloths etc.

4th day the 21st

Settled down to write for J.F. in the business

5th day the 22nd

Wrote for the business today also.

6th day the 23rd

In the morning we removed to fresh lodgings from the Merchants Hotel in Wall Street to Saidlers in Broadway the room being larger as also a more retired and pleasant situation.

7th day the 24th

In the forenoon having leasure I took a long walk

in the city and in the afternoon I wrote for the business.

1st day the 25th

I attended meeting both forenoon and after wherein several friends appeared in lively testimonies. It being the commencement of the Yearly Meeting for the State; the meeting houses were quite full and many had to stand out of doors, although here are two meeting houses one in Liberty Street and the other in Pearl Street; yet they both was not roomy enough to accomodate those that attended to sit down.

2nd day the 26th

J.F. gave up today to attend the Yearly Meeting which opened for discipline this morning and also gave me liberty at attend the same; which I did both sittings of the day to my great comfort and sattisfaction. The first sitting being the opening for business the time was much taken up with reading the Epistles from the other Yearly Meetings in the United States; as also one from Yearly meeting in London accompanied with a written salutation of love to their American bretheren, which appeared to me to be listened to with a degree of particular attention; and on which some religious remarks were made. Having now been about a week in this city and discussed its situation; for my own amusement I will note down the particulars as they have taken my attention viz. The city of New York appears to be built upon a neck of land almost surrounded by water commodiously situate for the large quantity of shipping that trade to it; being nearly equal to Liverpool in England. The houses of this city are now mostly of brick of an excellent quality the clay being tough and also well manufactured. The former houses were generally wood but the great and destructive fires have at one time or other nearly removed these sort of buildings out of sight. A fire that now happens to burn up an old wood house is called a benefit to the city as a new brick one is sure to be raised in its room, however this may not be pleasant to the owner of such premises. The streets are not much different to those of other towns excepting the rows of large trees of various kinds which grow on each side of many of the principal ones and in hot weather they are both pleasant and usefull especially in that called Broadway; it is rather elegant being of considerable length as also wide and ornamented with these spreading branch trees. Here are not many publick buildings in this city saving the town hall which is of white marble neatly worked. It overlooks a large open space of ground called the Park or rather a large grass plot. In this house the publick business is transacted, the mayor holds his court in it, with various other things which I am not acquainted with. The inhabitants are computed at from 120 to 130 thousand, a considerable number of coloured people included; they are well supplied with water though not of a very good quality; one or more pumps are put down in allmost every street especially in opening or meeting of the cross ones. New York is not how I have heard it represented an unarmed situation. In the bay as at Boston are several islands on which are built strong batteries on the top of one is a telegraph. The entrance to the habour is narrow so that it would require great strength and management for an enemy ship to do any damage to the city of New York.

3rd day the 27th

I again attended both the sittings of the meeting today in which the queries were gone through and the state of society considered. Many friends delivered weighty matter on the deficiences that appeared and at the close of the sitting a committee was chosen to draw up a salutation to the absent members.

4th day morning the 28th

A meeting for worship commenced at 10 o'clock A friend named Jesse Kersey spoke very animatedly upon the passage when the apostle Peter was sent for to the house of Cornelius and another man friend named Dr. Edward Atlee both from Philadelphia appeared in suplication so the meeting for worship closed having been a very favoured time. In the afternoon sitting Minutes of last year was read and those left for this Meetings consideration were gone through with some other little matters of business concerning friends schools. The meeting adjourned with reading a deceased woman friends Memorial which was accepted and agreed to be recorded.

5th day the 29th

Attended the morning sitting of the Yearly meeting in which was discussed a minute left of the books last year relative to persons marrying those not members of our society being immediately disowned for such offence. Several friends spoke weightily on the subject expressing the uneasiness it had caused and how very contrary it was to real gospel order. An eminent minister while speaking on the subject observed that in some cases it was the least offence a member of the society could be guilty of. The meeting appointed a committee to consider of something as an amendment to that rule respecting marriage. The next business that claimed the meetings attention was the schools established by friends with the management and select nature of them, which after adjourned to the 4th hour in the afternoon - which I attended. the committee appointed to prepare the general epistle brought the same in, which was read. It contained weighty and religious matter, a sufficient number of copies were ordered to be printed and sent down to the subordinate meetings. In this sitting also was read the minutes of the meeting for sufferings from last year. They contained accounts of a great many applications from quarterly meetings requesting assistance towards building new meeting houses; a proof of the increase of the society - also was read the copy of the address of the Legislature desiring that government would take into consideration those still held in slavery in the States. It appeared well adapted to the purpose and had met with a kind reception congress having enacted that a total emancipation should take place in the year 1827. Another minute was also read concerning the friends meetings in execution since last year. Some were finished, some in the press and the like. A memorial of a deceased woman friend was read and the meeting adjourned. Today I was informed by a person of respectability just arived from the State of Georgia that the harvest was commenced and the fields of wheat ready for reaping and not more than 840 miles from New York.

6th day the 30th

Attended both sittings of today which was almost whoely taken up with the Epistle brought in by the committees appointed for that purpose addressed to friends of the Yearly Meeting in London, also to the Yearly Meetings of Baltimore, Ohio and Carolina. Mary Nuttal the English woman friend on a religious visit to America had this day an opportunity with the men's meeting - so the meeting adjourned having nearly got through the business, a meeting at 8 o'clock to finish was appointed on the following morning.

7th day 5th month 31st

At 7 o'clock this morning we took our luggage on board the steam boat on our way to Philadelphia. She steered over the New York bay taking the route along the River Raritan the Stattan Island on our left and the Jersey shore on our right. The weather being fine the woodlands, rock etc. had a most beautiful appearance. At 10 o'clock the boat touched at a wharf near the village of Pearth Amboy; a pleasant situation where they usually land and take in passengers 30 miles from New York. Next place New Brunswick coaches meet the boat and take the passengers from thence overland to Trenton. After dining at Brunswick the place of the boat and coaches exchanging passengers we again took to the woods, which in this part grew large and high. The oak for shipbuilding is plentiful here. They cut down such timber and make it into rafts on the Delaware conveying the same to Philadelphia, New York etc. to the dock yards for the above purpose. Passed through Kingston a small clean village also through Princton and changed horses. At this place is a college and many young men appeared to be educating at this institution from thence onto Trenton where is a large wood bridge. It is supported by arches of wood overhead: carriages and passengers go through it, which has the appearance of going through a large building; having a roof erected over the whole construction both for preservation as well as a safeguard to keep horses from taking fright. This is over the River Delaware which parts the states of Jersey and Pensylvania. At Trenton we took an extra carriage and pushed on to Bristol which place we reached about 10 o'clock, distance from New York about 70 miles 30 of which we travelled by land through the wood country, the remaining 40 by the steam boat. Having lodged at Bristol another first day came on which was the

1st of the 6th month

This is also a small town most pleasantly situated on the banks of the Delaware river. After breakfast J.F. another friend and myself took a boat which ferried us over the river to Burlington about a mile accross on the opposite shore - a friends meeting being held at that place which we attended. It is a large gathering we understood about 60 families of friends belonged to this particular meeting. On its breaking up we went to George Dilwins to dinner; an old friend who had been in most parts of England. This is also a beautiful situation yet not large. About 4 o'clock we were taken onto the steam boat and proceeded down the Delaware. The prospect of each side is truly beautiful. green fields with here or there a clean looking house and garden that overlooks the river. We arrived at the city of Philadelphia about 7 o'clock in the evening and took up our lodging at the Washington Hotel, a large boarding house, having sailed from Bristol to this city in about 2 1/2 hours the distance near 21 miles which is in all from New York to Philadelphia by this route is computed at near 91 miles.

2nd day morning 6th month 2nd

Having now travelled over a great extent of the country I will note down their manner of cultivating which appears to be generally as follows. In the first place they will cut down say from 5 to 10 acres of wood, leaving the stumps of the trees standing above the surface of the ground about 18 or 20 inches. After clearing all off except these stumps they apply a small rooting plough drawn by 2 or 4 oxen and yet to observe how thick on the ground the stumps stand they will with these rooting irons tumble the earth over around them in an astonishing manner; afterwards sow rye or plant Indian corn which appears to be the main support as bread corn amongst the poorer sort of people. Then perhaps in about 2 or 3 years as these tree stumps become decayed with the weather they dig them out and the land may then be considered as arable. The manner of fencing is also very simple; they are nothing more than poles piled in a certain form upon each other something like the following which if piled high enough make a very good enclosure; hundreds of acres are done in this way having neither pin nor nail about them. Today I kept pretty much in the house writing and straightening our cloths etc. I noticed in passing about that French is a very common language at Philadelphia both poor and rich seem to speak French.

3rd day the 3rd

Having leasure today I took several walks about the city. It is large and magnificent - the founder William Pen gives the plan of Philadelphia in his works which is still adhered to. The streets take their origin at the river Delaware and extend backwards in a straight direction into the country;

The diary page below contains a drawing relating to the manner of fencing used in which poles were piled in a certain form upon each other.

with the cross streets in regular order - say the river Delaware runs along the east of the city; where the streets take their rise to westward and the transversal ones are north and south, forming squares or right angles, the central street is called Market Street, being nearly in the centre of the city up the middle of which is built a colonade market place; here farmers, butchers, gardeners, fish-mongers etc. may expose their goods with convenience and advantage under cover. The street on each side of this market is wide and commodious, this street being the central line the other streets take their names from it viz north, south 1st 2nd 3rd 4th north or south street. This city enjoys a great privilege over other large places both in America and elsewhere; having plenty of room both in the streets and also in gardens and backyards. Here is also another most valuable advantage which is the great river Delaware; its water being fresh and of particular good quality, this is not the case with sea port towns in general. The following is in some sort

The drawing below shows the manner in which Delaware was laid out in blocks. The River Delaware is shown at the lower edge of the drawing.

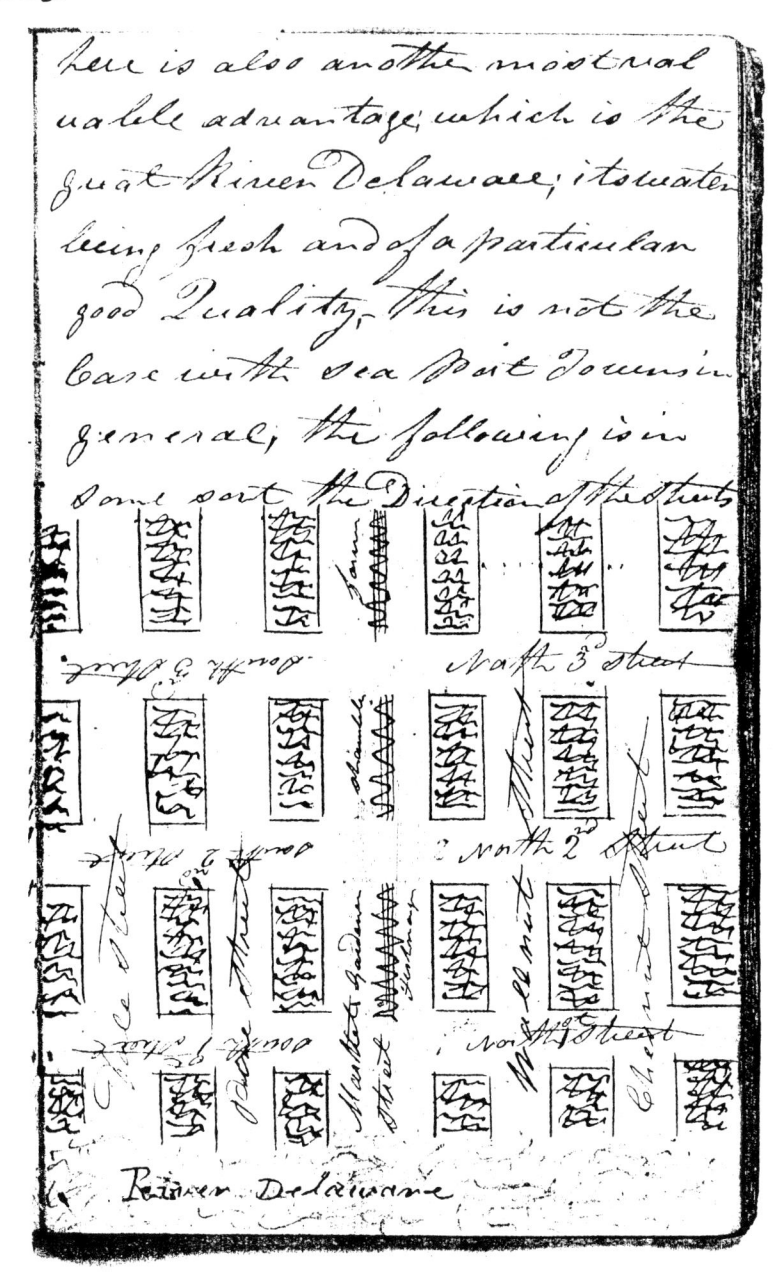

the direction of the streets. The houses are mostly brick, the publick buildings fronted with white marble. The inhabitants are computed at from 90 to a hundred thousand; not so numerous as at New York yet to appearance a great deal more extensive a city. Here is not so much shipping at this place as at New York; consequently not so much publick business, although large vessels may conveniently lay to the pearhead. The state house in Philadelphia has been deservedly spoken of by travellers. It is a rather large but ancient building, the publick business of the city is transacted in it, Justice Courts with many other affairs of that sort are settled in the different appartments. Within this building is a most extensive and valuable museum; the property of Willson Peale; the collection of curiosities is far beyond anything I ever saw of the sort. The enourmous Mammouth's skeleton is exhibited standing in full proportion, it measures 18 feet in length 11ft.5 inches high, its limb head and tusk bone are in the same monstrous proportion; the very sight of which cannot fail to strike the mind with awefull sensations. I cannot tell how to describe it (see the 40th and 41st chapter of the book of Job) well except by inserting here the translation of the Indian Tradition which is as follows:

"Ten thousand moons ago when nought but gloomy forests covered this land of the sleeping sun; long before the pale men with thunder and fire at their command rushed on the wings of the wind to ruin this garden of nature; when naught but the untamed wanderers of the woods and men as unrestrained as they were the lords of the soil; a race of animals existed, huge as the frowning precipice, cruel as the bloody panther swift as the descending eagle and terrible as the angel of night. The pines crashed beneath their feet and the lake shrunk when they slaked their thirst; the forcefull javelin in vain was hurled and the barbed arrow fell harmless from their sides. Forests were laid waste at a meal, the groans of expiring animals were everywhere heard, and whole villages inhabited by men were destroyd in a moment, the cry of universal distress extending even to the region of peace in the west, and the good spirit interposed to save the unhappy. The forked lightening gleamed around and loudest thunder rocked the globe. The bolts of heaven were hurled upon the cruel destroyers alone and the mountains echoed with the bellowings of death. All were killed except one male, the fiercest of the race, and him even the artillery of the skies assailed in vain, he ascended the bluest summit which shades the source of the Monangahela, and roaring aloud bid defiance to every vengeance. The red lightening scorched the lofty firs and ruined the knotty oaks but only glanced upon the enraged monster. At length maddened with fury he leaped over the waves of the west at a bound and this moment reigns the uncontrolled monarch of the wilderness, in despite of even Omnipotence itself." Under the head of this huge skeleton in a small glass box is that of a mouse, showing the contrast of the two once living animals. Here is in the same room in waxwork etc. men of the different savage Indian tribes and other nations of the wild sort of people; in their native dress and I believe in figure and colour a striking resemblance. These stand in full proportion with their badges of honour and weapons of war; I counted one dress with near 30 marks or significations, of certainty that the living warrior had slain the same number of persons and taken their scalps. They appear ferocious beyond description. Here is also other large bones and skeletons which have been found in many parts of the world. Also large wild beasts, birds and fishes with serpants, shells etc. from every known quarter of the globe. Metals and mineral of all kinds in their natural state, outlandish weapons of war and dress. Amongst the rest is a piece of Mary Dyers gown who laid down her life at Boston for the principals of what she believed was true religion. It is a light drab worsted stuff, as also a piece of the bed curtain fringe of William Penns bed which he lodged in when about settling the State of Pensylvania with a great many curious carvings and inscriptions found underground in different parts of the earth both on wood, stone and metal, with a very great variety of ancient and rare matters of antiquity that I cannot recollect. Willson Peale is an elderly person near 70 years of age. He is esteemed a great natural philosopher and has I understand been a collector of curious antiquities most part of his life, he is the proprietor of the before mentioned museum.

4th day the 4th

In the forenoon I wrote for the business, in the evening took a walk about the city. I observed that the trees in the streets were not quite so common as in those of New York and yet a few large ones grow in some of the outermost streets of the city. Ornaments of this kind are suffered to grow less or more in most of the American cities and in the smaller towns more so.

5th day the 5th

Packed up our luggage and at 1 o'clock embarked on board the steam boat on our way to Baltimore; at about 3 o'clock touched at Chester where is a settlement of friends, at 5 o'clock passed Marcas Hook, afterwards Wilmington and at 7 o'clock reached our destination of Newcastle about 40 miles by water on the Delaware river. This is a small town on the river bank where the stages meet the steam boat and exchange passengers and luggage.

6th day the 6th

Now in the state of Delaware. Having lodged at Newcastle we at 4 o'clock arose and took to the stage which conveyed us overland through the State of Delaware and into part of the State of Maryland to a small village called Frenchtown at the head of the Elk river which place the English landed in the war with the United States, put the people and garrison to flight and burned down a military store kept there. The steam boat called the Chesapeake was waiting for us at the head of this river on which we embarked about 1/2 past 7 o'clock having come from Newcastle in the stages, 5 in number a distance of about 16 miles. About 9 o'clock we sailed across the entrance of Bohemia river, at 11 passed the mouth of the Susqueanna river into the Chesapeake Bay which is large. Here the steam boat steered by the compass and about 5 o'clock we entered the Patapasco river that runs to Balimore at which place we arrived about 7 o'clock in the evening - distance from Frenchtown 75 miles and total from Philadelphia by this route called the best one, 131 miles. Being now arrived at the city of Baltimore we took up our lodgings at the Fountain Inn.

7th day 6th month the 7th

After putting our things a little to rights in the morning, I in the afternoon took my walks about the city. It is built in the newer part of Wm. Pens plan much like Philadelphia but in the old parts the streets are crooked and narrow. The inhabitants are supposed to be about 70 thousand. Trees are not quite as common in the streets here as at New York and Philadelphia. Black people are more numerous at this place than in any other part we have previously been at. It is painful to observe how many there are still held as slaves in this city and parts adjacent - and there are persons at present in Baltimore who have dealings in this shocking business - yet a great part of the thinking sober people set their faces against it as much as possible, so that a slave dealer dare not have himself known to be such if by any means he can help it. The river Patapasco runs to this place and a neck of land stands into the river a short distance from the city, which forms a good and safe habour. A fort is also built upon it guarded by soldiers to protect the place when at war with other nations. Today the weather was fine and hot.

1st day the 8th

At 10 o'clock J.F. and myself went to Meeting. Friends have two meeting places in this city. We were informed that about 250 families of friends reside at Baltimore amongst whom are several valuable ministers. In the afternoon also attended meeting.

2nd day the 9th

Being a wet day I kept house and attended on J.F. with other little matters of writing. In the evening I took a walk out of the city. Everything looked green and pleasant in the vegitable world.

3rd day the 10th

Stoped pretty much in the house and attended on some little matters for J.F. Shower of rain.

4th day the 11th

Went to meeting in the morning and afterwards walked through the market which is held on 4th and 6th day. Flour sold at 60 dollars a barrel of 196 lbs., beef at about 10 cts. mutton at 8 cts. and veal at 9 cts. Strawberries cherries and early fruit in plenty. The lower classes of people here are to appearance mostly Africans - scarsely an European servant is to be seen in any house - either friends or others. In the afternoon having leasure I took a walk to the signal house. It is built upon a high hill on the south side of the harbour about half a mile from the city, from whence may be seen the situation of Baltimore with the bay and surrounding country. the prospect is undeniably pleasant. This observatory commands a view of the wide river Patapasco towards the sea as far as the eye can reach and if assisted with the telescope vessels can be discovered a good days sail from the wharf.

5th day the 12th

About a 1/4 mile from Baltimore is a publick well of water called the city spring which I this day visited it is a most beautiful place, the well is several feet below the surface of the ground down to which is a flight of white marbel steps. The water runs through 3 pipes about 1 1/2 inch bore into a marbel trough and overflows down a channel nearby hewn in the same material, then over the whole constructions is built a large circular arched shed, erected upon lofty pillars and overhung with high broad leafd trees altogether makes a compleet and beautiful watering place, the water of itself is of a peculiar good quality. The citizens are setting up two marble monuments to the memory of President George Washington one in the town and the other in the edge of the wood on the north side of the city, a great many work people are employed in this business. A gin or horse mill is erected at the large monument on purpose to saw and scower the marble, it will be a good many months before they can be finished and will cost a great sum of money which some people would prefer being spent in more useful purposes. I also attended friends weekday meeting at the east end of town it is not quite so large as that held on 4th day at the west end. An old woman friend expressed herself in a very feeling and religious manner concerning the deciples of our Lord formerly when they were with one accord assembled and the doors were shut; that their blessed master stood in the midst and consolingly said peace unto you, the subject itself, with the weighty manner in which it was delivered had I trust a good effect on minds present.

6th day the 13th

Attended on J.F. doing business and writing. Today the weather was fine and hot with a clear atmosphere. A person at our Inn from the state of Verginia expressed that he did not remember ever being more opressed with heat than on this day 6th month 13th although he resided near 200 miles south of Baltimore. At this place in the hot weather people have recourse to the mineral waterhouses of which there are several in this city. They consist of a small room in the front street beautifully set out with carpets, sofas and flowers fresh from the gardens; with anything that has a cooling appearance, soda water with other cooling and chemical drinks are sold in these rooms. They have for their sign in large gilt letters over the door the Fountain of Hygeia. These are very usefull places so people get the wholesome and cooling beverage instead of going to the gin shops and drinking liquors of a more heating nature.

7th day the 14th

Wrote home to my wife as also for the business. Today clear atmosphere and very hot.

1st day the 15th

Attended meetings at East end in the morning and West end in the evening. Today north west wind and more cooling.

2nd day the 16th

Today kept within doors pretty much and wrote for the business.

3rd day the 17th

In the morning wrote for J.F. and attended on business and at 6 o'clock we took steam boat and started our return towards Philadelphia. the evening fine with wind southerly.

4th day the 18th

At about 4 o'clock this morning we reached French Town after a tossing night in the Chesapeake Bay. We has 45 passengers on board amongst whom were several wimmen. The water being a little rough it affected the females so that many of them became very sick and the night was also hot which made it all together an unpleasant passage. the stages now conveyed us overland to Newcastle where the Philadelphia steam boat was ready to receive us at this place. Yesterday was a great uproar occasioned by three white or European men who had been long noted for stealing or rather kidnapping the black people whether free or slaves and sending them on small slave ships into the State of Georgia sold for life, they were clearly found out as follows; They siezed upon a stout free black man who after a severe struggle was obliged to yield to their three superior strengths. They took from him his watch and most other things he had about his person and sold him into the State of Georgia, but very favourable to himself he had his manumission rolled up close in the bottom of his watch pocket which they did not discover, and in the course of time after being sold for life and robbed both of what property he had about him; as also of his freedom; he one day met with one of his aquaintance a person who happened to be travelling in that part of the country; to whom he made himself and his case known, at the same time showing him his paper of release, the person immediately took up the matter and had him free, and the next they got authority and took of these three noted men stealers, the case was so clearly proved against them that the court at Newcastle found them guilty and sentanced them to be flogged to stand in the pillory, which I saw, as also to have the lower part of their ears cut off which was done at Newcastle afforesaid on 3rd day 17th of 6th month 1817 greatly to the joy of the poor suffering Africans who assembled in great numbers to see these three, their great enemies so justly suffer for crimes so heinous and yet so common in this land of liberty (as it is called) the Eagle's Eye hath not penetrated to this point so fully as is desirable to the full emancipation of the African race in this country. We were now embarked on board the steam boat again and had a fine sail up the Delaware, landing a second time at the city of Philadelphia about one o'clock on this day being 4th day, 6th month 18th, 1817.

DIARY THREE

5th day 6th month 19th

Stopped in house and wrote for the business most of the day.

6th day the 20th

Spent the day much the same as yesterday the weather very hot and much lightening in the evening and night.

7th day the 21st

Having now taken a good deal of notice of the weather etc. since J.F. and myself arrived in this country I will here insert some of my general observations viz: The spring comes later than in England owing to the long and severe hard frosts which prevail in the winter, say the American spring does not commence until 5th month May when the farmers begin to plant their Indian corn etc. at which season the sun gets high with alternate changes of warm and wet days which starts the vegitation more at once than in England. In the 6th month June the climate and firmament has a very different appearance altogether to that of Yorkshire in England for instance daylight in a morning is not till 4 o'clock the day seems to begin nearer at the sunrise and the sky at the horizon seems to be more direct upright the firmament also appears to be at a much greater distance from the earth. At 12 o'clock noon the sunshine to a persons thinking even overhead and if clear from cloud at this season it feels to bite through the cloths upon the top of ones sholders, the calves of the legs and other exposed parts of the body. If the wind blow southerly lightening mostly commences at sunset which on this day appeared to be about 8 o'clock and in half an hour afterwards it was quite dark, the evening not being particularly overcast so that the longest day in America may be computed from 4 o'clock in the morning to 8 o'clock in the evening, sixteen hours. The longest day in England is much longer than in America say two full hours at least. The sun in this country seems to run at this time of year a more straight and direct course not so circuitous as in Yorkshire in England, hence it follows that the mother country is favoured with more twilight which lengthens their day so much more than in America. This evening came on heavy rain lightening and thunder yet being the longest day we had occasion for candles to write by as early as 8 o'clock. I am informed that the day here on the shortest day is much longer than ours in England. Variations of this kind with other alterations which I observe to take place in the climate while in this country I will endeavour to keep proper memorandums of them in this way for my own government at a future period, as also for my children and the amusement of my friends.

1st day the 22nd

J.F. and myself attended meeting in Pine Street. The house was nearly full and being very warm weather I felt very much oppressed from the heat and had a very uncomfortable sitting, at the close of which I thought I had not been so overspent since my arrival in this country. So far as I have noticed in all the places I have been here, the inhabitants pay great regard for the sabbath day, it is pleasant to observe such numbers of people going to their separate meeting houses, friends with most other societies seem to go at the same hour which has a pleasing appearance to a stranger and a wellwisher to the cause of religion, to see the streets at the hours of meeting time, how they are filled with clean orderly people of the different denominations all quietly walking etc. to their places of worship. Attended same meeting in the evening still very warm and close

2nd day the 23rd

The wind westerly this morning and rather cooler. We on our return from Baltimore took our lodging as before at the Washington Hotel a very large boarding house; much more comfortable than the Fountain Inn at Baltimore, yet this house is also infested with swarms of great biting flies, though not quite so numerous as at the Baltimore Fountain. There we had thousands and tens of thousands. This Philadelphian mansion house or the Washington Hotel is considered the head lodging place for travellers from almost every part of Europe resort to this house while visiting the city and of course a veriaty of languages may be heard among the guests. Their mealtimes are punctual as follows: Breakfast at 8, dinner at 3 tea at six and supper at nine o'clock at which time, when the meal is on the table one of the waiters rings a large bell; while another beats an Egyptian gong with a stick much like a big drum stick with a ball at the end. This gong is suspended by a string in the passage of the house. It measures 24 inches over. It has the appearance of a sieve or small boiler bottom; being turned up at the sides about 2 inches; it seems to be a mixture of metals of copper, brass tin etc. the colour in the bright parts is that of a whitish brass. It is also marked with foreign characters. When hit with the bale stick it makes a very large jarring and dreadful noise, so much so that while beating the building shakes with its harsh sound. In the evening being more cool and pleasant I took a walk to the village of Kensington 2 1/2 miles from the city of Philadelphia. It has all the appearance of a country situation, perhaps 3/4 of a mile of farmhouses with open green or common before them. The river Delaware runs all along the back of this town and on which rafts of timber are floated here for ship builders who are stationed in the docks about this village. Kensington is the place where formerly grew the large elm tree under which William Penn made his treaty with the Indian natives previous to his settling the State of Pensylvania. This tree has been blown down some years ago yet at this present time there remaineth several yards of its stumps prostrate on the ground, which is hewn and cut in various places by strangers who from curiosity and the notedness of it, have taken pieces to different parts of the globe myself amongst the rest: as I split a piece of this tree with my own hand the perfixed is a part of it.

The diary page below shows the strips of bark taken from the stumps of the Elm tree mentioned above. The strips were held in position by sealing wax.

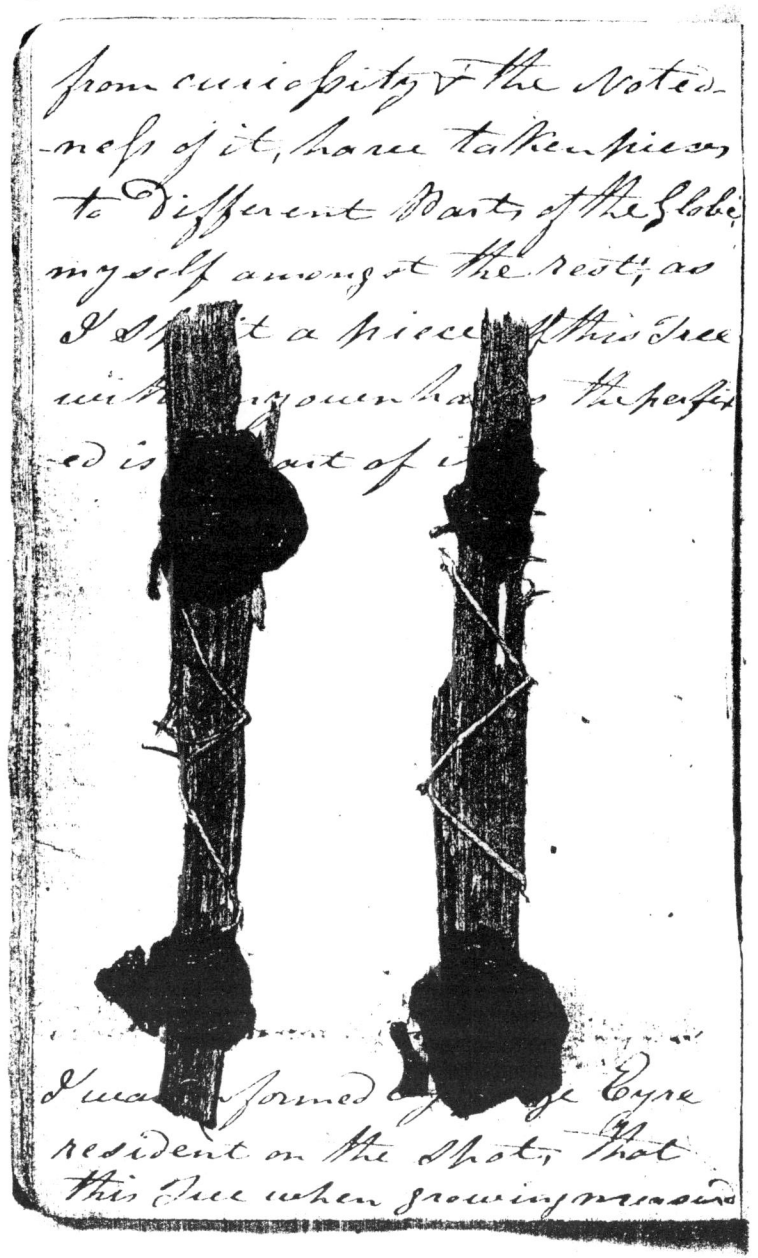

I was informed by George Eyre resident on the spot, that this tree when growing measured round the thick part of bole 21 feet, the height and branches were also prodigious. G.E. told me that his goats would have run up its bole and all up and down amongst its branches while growing; also a very pleasant summer house was built in it. It seems to be a good stones cast away from the river's brink. George Eyre, the person before named who lives very near to where the tree grew, presented me with a piece of it, cut off the edge of a plank, a number of which he has still in reserve and gives pieces away to the curious and travellers who come to view the spot where the bargin was made between William Penn and the Indians for the State of Pensylvania.

3rd day 6th month 24th

This morning the wind north and west more cool and pleasant. In the evening I walked as far out of the city as to the river Schuylkill. The country here is very beautiful, adorned with genteel situations, green fields and woodlands. At the entrance into the city from this part is a circle of grass plot or plantation in which stands a female figure upon some rough rock wood surrounded by a pool of water and a variety of shrubs,

This painting shows the signing of Penn's treaty with the Indians. To the right is the tree from the stump of which John Adamson stripped some bark for inclusion in his diary. (Reproduced by courtesy of The Pennsylvania Academy of Fine Arts - Gift of Mrs. Sarah Harrison : The Joseph Harrison Jr. Collection)

amongst which rise up 10 small streams of water to the height of 20 feet which falls around this figure into the pool again. She holds upon her shoulder some kind of sea bird which also spouts up water to a great height. This is a most beautiful sight especially in hot weather. It is situate at the end of Market Street at the entrance of the city. Tonight I observed one of Robert Sutcliffe's remarks confirmed respecting the farmers waggons and horses lodging out in the open street. I counted from 30 to 40 of these carriages in this situation. The waggons are large and covered with bows or ribs of canvas, narrow wheels and invariably drawn by a pole and most generally 5 horses. The driver always rides on the last one and has a rein to the lead horse. These wagons come from one to four hundred miles out of the country; they bring flower, leather etc. Whether on the road or in the towns or city when night comes they loose out the horses and sets the carriage across the road or street backed to the side, then fixes the manger which they take along with them upon the pole in front of the waggon

Depicting the 4th of July celebrations in Centre Square, Pennsylvania, this picture also shows the fountain mentioned in John Adamson's diaries. (Reproduced by courtesy of The Pennsylvania Academy of Fine Arts - purchased from the estate of Paul Beck Jr.)

so the horses stand each side of this manger, the same as in ever so good a stable. The geering is hung up in order about the carriage. I was informed that winter or summer this is their regular mode of lodging, yet in the severe weather it must be very trying as the winters in this country are very inclement at times. I notice their horses to be both fine and in very good condition.

4th day the 25th

In the forenoon wrote for the business; attended to the post office and other matters on the trades account. In the evening crossed the Delaware in the vessel that is plied by 9 horses instead of steam unto the Jersey shore. The land that side the river appears to be rich. The Indian corn seems to flourish very much in the state of Jersey. The Delaware is about a mile over from Philadelphia to the Jersey shore, and on the team boat they charge a foot passenger what they call a 5 penny bit, a piece of silver worth 6 1/4 cents or about our 3d sterling. On this boat coaches with the driver and those inside the coach drive onto the boat and there sit in there places same as on land during the time the vessel is propeling over, and when to shore they drive off with the greatest composure, farmers carts and waggons loaded and unloaded are in the same way conveyed across this river with numbers of foot passengers, and what surprises me most is that horses of the greatest spirit when they are on the water stand very still. I have seen horses ferried over in small open boats and yet stood as still as a stock. They appear to me to know their situation when on the water as do other dumb creatures, a fowl or dog when let loose on shipboard on the sea will not fly nor jump overboard.

5th day 6th month 26th

The weather in general is more hot in America than in England in the summers and more cold in the winter. I observe the people in the winter lay up a stock of ice to use in summer, the great houses have all an Ice House; It is very useful for instance their butter in summer would soon melt had they not means to prevent it. When it is set on the table a piece of ice is laid upon it, or put in a tin and the butter place sat upon that. Also to make their water or wine drink cold they put in a piece of ice which makes it very cold almost immediately. They also keep their shambles meat in these ice houses with other things they wish to preserve cool. In the afternoon we went to see the state prison which was certainly a great treat. This house of confinement now contains 676 prisoners viz 470 convicted and 206 to take their trials. We were informed that by the English laws out of these 470 convicts near 300 of the cases would have been punished with death, but here they have another method by obliging them to work for a longer or shorter term as their crime may be, very seldom punishing with death except in cases of premeditated murder. At a stranger first going into the prison it has the appearance of different tradespeople being all busy at work, which in reality is so for instance masons and labourers sawing and rubbing stone and marble, shoe makers, taylors, painters, shipbuilders, weavers, linen and woollen, boys carding and spinning, furriers, joiners, whitesmiths, blacksmiths etc. all at work as if at their own homes yet no doubt they feel their situation. Being prisioners of all trades they are able to make and manufacture etc. everything they want, in short we were informed by the managers that the place supported itself, they do everything within themselves viz. washing, baking, brewing etc., the women prisoners of which there are a great many do all the washing ironing, mending etc. We noticed a great many very bad countenances especially amongst the men, several of whom, who had been refractory were confined to their cells and ironed. I observed a great many black people prisoners both men boys and women. In one of the Keepers rooms hung a picture, a female figure representing friendship exploring the iron grating of a prison, an English naval officer who was confined for forgery had composed the following lines wrote at the bottom of the above picture viz:

At the door of a prison see friendship in tears

May her object some pity inspire

May the hand of humanity banish her fears

And relieve while it stoops to admire

Tis an emblem which mortals may view with
                              delight

May divinity brighten the scene

Twas to save when from heaven our lord
                              took his flight

To pardon and cleanse the unclean.

By John Lewis Calvert, Lieut. in the British Navy. This is a very striking painting and greatly impressed my mind with the awefullness of a prison.

6th day the 27th

In the forenoon wrote on the business account and in the evening I went with some friends to see the hospital or Asylum. It is a beautiful situation nearly out of the city at the end of the south 8th street. In the corner of the house stands upon a pillar of marble a statue of William Penn in Bronze in full proportion holding in his left hand the charter and pointing to it with his other as follows. Charter of Privileges to Pennsylvania NDCC Almighty God being the only lord of conscience I do grant and declare that no person who shall acknowledge one Almighty God; and profess himself only obliged to live quietly and under the civil government shall be in any case molested, - William Penn born 1644 died 1718 - this wrote on the pillor as also the seal or coat of arms the figure of a lion inscribed Mercy and Justice - Pennsylvania granted by Charles the second to William Penn in 1681, He arrived in America in 1682 made a just and amicable arrangement with the natives for the purchase of their lands and went back to England in 1684, returned to Pensylvania in 1699 and finally withdrew to his paternal estates in 1701. In the gardens of this institution are growing orinages lemon and grapes in the open air in abundance. There was a great many patients as at other houses of this kind; the visit was upon the whole agreeable and interesting.

7th day the 28th

This day spent pretty much in reading. J.F. going out into the country with some friends to visit an establishment much the same as the retreat at York.

6th month the 29th

Being first day I attended meetings: Arch Street in the morning and Pine Street in the evening the former is a very large gathering but the latter more select and agreeable at the close of which I took a little walk out of the city with cousen Joseph Sharp. We observed some very fine wheat which appeared to be ripining pretty fast - thought about 8 days of fine weather would make it ready for reaping.

2nd day 6th month 30th

Today a westerly wind and very clean and fine. I did very little on anything but read with a walk towards evening. J.F. went out with some friends.

3rd day 7th month 1st

Wrote part of today and took a walk to the wood wharfs, a load drawn by one horse is about what they call half a coard and when led up into the city and sawed ready to lay on the fire it costs 3 dollars 25 cents Sterling 14/7 1/2. It will last on one fire in moderate weather say from 3 weeks to a month. Coals of a poorish kind sell at about 2/- sterling a bushel but very few are used, wood being prefered. Here is great quantities of it brought up the river out of the states of Delaware and Maryland to Philadelphia when at one time or another it is certain to be sold.

4th day the 2nd

Being a hot day I stoped in house pretty much. JF going out on a visit to stop all night, so having little to attend to I rested myself and read a little.

5th day the 3rd

Attended meeting at Arch Street to my satisfaction and in the afternoon wrote on business. In the evening JH an English man from Manchester invited me to go with him to hear a lecture delivered upon gass, which I accepted. It was at Willson Peale's museum which was lighted up with the same, he showed us many usefull demonstrations in the above science. When about retiring to bed one of our boarders came in saying Gentlemen I have just been robbed, his name was Eyde just arrived from the West Indies. He had borrowed a horse of N. Renshaw the Keeper of our house, to ride to Frankfort about 8 miles from the city to visit one of his friends and when returning in the evening within about 2 1/2 miles of town a person on the road before him appeared to be walking gently along. When he was just about to ask him if he was in the right way to the city as being a stranger but before he had time to articulate the sentence, the man before darted suddenly across the road and clicked the bridle; at the same moment with the other hand holding a pistol close up to his brest saying deliver or I will blow your brains out. Our boarder who was a very stout man but being taken so at unawares without either stick or weapon of any sort to defend himself with concluded it best to give up what he had about him, whereupon he desired the villians, as a second was now come up, not to take his life and he would quietly give them what he had, which as it happened was as near as he could recollect about 8 or 10 dollars, declaring to them it was all he had about him, but they not satisfied with that said we must search you, so the one undertook while he was on horseback to feel in his pockets and about the outside of his cloths, the other still holding the horse and pistol close to him, so when they had got what he had which he at the first gave up to them, they grumblingly let go of his horse. He being now a little more composed accosted them with saying as I don't know you being an entire stranger here, and as you have taken from me all that I had, will you tell me if I be in the right road to the city, upon which one of them answered you are and walked off, leaving him to make the best of his way which he accordingly did and in less than a mile met a carriage with a man and a woman in it, to whom he gave the information that he had met with two footpads, who had taken his money from him. the person in the carriage asked him if they were armed to which he informed they were. However the carriage proceeded and he also made home as fast as he could. He arrived at the Washington Hotel about 10 o'clock or perhaps a half hour after, and related the circumstances in my hearing.

6th day the 4th

Today is what the Americans call the fourth of July which they celebrate with festivity being the day of which they declared their independance, a number of old men who had been active supporters for this independance several of whom had been in battle had a dinner provided at our house in a separate room to themselves. Two of above persons came and sat down in the room I was in and fell to discourse of battles and straits they had gone through in the first revolutionary war with England. I overheard them relate a many remarkable occurances in which their lives were at stake and one of them, an old grey headed man argued that it certainly was not from or by their own strength that they became masters of the country but a providential permission alliging that the English might have cut them entirely up at various times had they proceeded at which times perhaps as he related in seasons of particular danger a great fog or heavy rain would fall in their favour and he himself had witnessed particular preservation one time above the rest, being on the look out with two horsemen his attendents. They were surprised by the British - his horseman behind fled and left him to his fate, the British officer was within a few yards of him he turning round his horse galloped off, the English calling out to him to stop on pain of being immediately shot if he persisted. However, he still kept up his speed whereupon the English officer ordered two of the best horses and men to persue him and after 3 or 4 miles of chase they came up with him one on each side charging him to stand or they would dispatch him in a moment with their swords. However at the moment one struck him violently with his sword and wounded him severely at the same instant he drew his pistol and shot the other through the brest and before the first one could raise his sword to bring a second blow he caught him by the arm and sword tassel taking his surviving antagonist a sudden blow in the face with the cock of his pistol which sunk into his nose and forehead the blood gushing out of the wound at the same moment; almost covered them both. He had now nearly subdued both these British horsemen when the remainder of the English troop came up. He was again obliged to gallop off which he instantly did and quite cleared himself of the enemy and got safe with his life to the camp of his own troops although very much wounded. The above conversation I overheard between two old generals as I pretended to be reading, yet was at same time attending their discourse. The one still holds a generalship in the army but the other who had witnessed the foregoing was a citizen. I spent the day pretty much in writing on the business account.

7th day the 5th

Attended on some little matters for JF and in the evening I bathed in the Delaware in a machine constructed for that purpose, the water cool and refreshing which I thought of use to me.

1st day the 6th

Attended meeting in Arch Street in the morning, but being so very hot and a thunder storm commenced at the afternoon meeting time I stoped in house and read in my bible. When the storm was over it was more agreeably cool which to me was very acceptable as the heat in the meeting in the forenoon was certainly very oppressive.

2nd day the 7th

Today employed in the business the weather very hot.

3rd day the 8th

Had some conversation with George Stephenson, a person resident at Pittsburgh West of Philadelphia on the Ohio river about 298 miles the outside of Pensylvania State. He informed me that land in that neighbourhood (say from 10 to 20 miles round) sold for about 18 dollars an acre on an average, part of which with moderate management would produce 12 to 20 bushels of wheat per acre and a farm of 200 acres the whole of the taxation would not amount to more than 5 dollars Sterling 22/6d - the above farm in fair cultivation not more wood than is convenient for fire fuel and other improvements - the climate healthy and agreeable. Today wrote for the business attended to the post office etc.

4th day the 9th

Spent the day pretty much in reading with some other little business that fell out.

5th day the 10th

In the evening of yesterday as JF was returning from a friends house where he had been paying a visit he was accosted by some boys in the street saying sir here is yonder a person stealing a black boy whereupon JF interested himself so much at the moment as also this morning by going to the magistrate etc. that the boy will now be likely to get a release and sent to his propper home. I went to the meeting in Arch Street today and afterwards called in Benjamen Kites Book Store and purchased Robert Sutcliffes travels in America for 8 dollars 25 cents the only copy left. While in conversation with this friend he informed me that fifteen hundred families of friends members of our society reside in the city of Philadelphia at the present time and as before observed they have five large meeting houses which on first days are very numerously attended with those not in membership together with the members causes the meeting houses to be very crowded which in hot weather is to an English person very oppresive. Today the wind blew from North East and in the evening became very cold, I thought more so than I had ever felt it since my arrival in America. A great change in a few days being on first day so overpressing hot that I could scarsely bear to walk out to meeting.

6th day the 11th

Wrote and attended on business.

7th day the 12th

Yesterday we got information of several arrivals both at New York and this place, about 8 o'clock this morning JF recieved letters from the former as expected one enclosed from P&G with information that a parcel was arrived by the late ship Minerva as also a letter from home, from J.Beaumont saying letters from our wives was in the parcel but being rather large they P&G thought it best to detain it until we arrived at New York ourselves, they having had previous information of our intentions of reaching that city in a few days. This was rather a disappointment to me, not having recieved any letter from my wife since the first one and now to understand one was waiting for me at New York made me anxious to leave Philadelphia for the present. Today I was pretty well employed in the business, the weather was also very hot. I this evening observed what the Americans call a fire fly - it has the appearance of sparks of fire upon the ground and in the air where they fly about like sparks over the top of a chimney when the soot is on fire.

1st day the 13th

Attended the north meeting in the morning to a good degree of satisfaction and in my way home accompanied by cousen Joseph Sharp, we steped on board a large ship just arrived from Amsterdam with four hundred and nine passengers, mostly German and Dutch peasantry, with a few mechanicks, a great many young men with several whole families consisting of their old men and wimmen mothers and fathers and small children. The bulk of these passengers were poor labouring people who as may be presumed had been obliged to emigrate for want of employment and the necessarys of life, and a great many of which had not a shilling to start with but had engaged with the captain for their passage on condition that when arriving in America they would engage themselves for a term, get their masters to advance for the captain the money due to him for their passage, fair etc. as they might be indebted. This scene was truly affecting, the ship was crowded in every part as may be supposed, being 409 passengers besides the ships crew, of the former we observed a great diversity of the rural dress customs, dialogue etc. etc. of these people, come no doubt from the remote corners of Holland and Germany to seek for themselves and families a maintenance in this wide and thinly inhabited country. It had in some measure the appearance of a slave vessel, a seaman being stationed at the mouth of the gangway with a drawn sword to guard any passenger escaping on shore who was under engagement with the captain for their passage etc. yet this seemed to be very proper in this case, as it would be very hard for the captain to have brought a person over and found him in meat during the passage after which to run away - no doubt there was of this description in the cargo. People who wanted servants had only to go on board and look round and pick out such as they liked, then to set about bargaining with them and the captain for their passages and fare. I think they had been 56 days on the passage, yet without much sickness saving 3 or 4 children had taken the smallpox. I was a little astonished at this their favour (as they in general) appeared very nasty and lousy in the extreme, several of the young men seemed anxious to be liberated. On our first going on deck they begun to arrange themselves standing upright showing us their stout manly stature etc. some having perhaps father and mother to treat for them and maybe the entire family would engage if wanted. This was certainly an interesting visit, having a tendancy to humble the mind and lead to the adoration of him who bestows his tender mercies upon us, who are so forgetfull and undeserving. I noticed several of these people eating something that appeared mean and worse by far than our English pig meat. Their dress was also coarse and shabby, the up-grown persons had very long hair some platted in two or three dirty looking tails dangling about the sholders the women wore some sort of a coloured cap being a narrow piece of cotton like cloth about 3 or 4 inches broad which they tied over the head and under the chin, leaving the back part of the head and neck bare, the hare being platted reaching down to the middle of the back yet in an untidy loose dirty manner. The old women in particular had a very disgusting appearance to an Englishman not accustomed to such manners. In the afternoon I went to see cousin Rebecca Sharp sister to John and Joseph Sharp, she came over into this country along with her brother Joseph about a year ago and now resides with AB as a nursemaid in this city. She is an active young woman and seems to have no prospect of returning to England. Cousin Joseph and myself took a little walk in the evening and passed an african meeting house just as the assembly was breaking up. It had an odd appearance, a large gathering of religious people with never a white person amongst them that I observed. On our return we were disented by an alarm of fire, fire and I believe a false alarm to exercise the fire men and engineers of whom there are several companies in Philadelphia. The alarm is given by men with speaking trumpets running about the city crying out fire, fire at such a place. The water engine and firemen where ever they be or how they may be circumstanced day or night if in health and within the sound of trumpet must immediately repair to their engine with the same to the place of fire. This we saw performed this evening with a degree of life and dexterity that was very diverting, the men were principally what are called young gentlemen with a short coarse drab jacket and a kind of cap signifying what company and engine they belong to. Most of the respectable houses have a number of leather buckets which are lent out in cases of this kind to supply the engines. Establishments of this sort are in great perfection in America, they having suffered so very much by fire in former years from so many of their old houses being built so entirely of wood.

2nd day the 14th

Did very little today - wrote and read with a short walk or two to the wharf. The wind northerly and a very calm and pleasant day.

3rd day the 15th

This morning we packed up our things and at 1 o'clock took a steam boat for New York, passing up the Delaware the scenary of both sides was truly beautiful, the day being clean and fine with a cooling northerly wind - the corn fields on each hand appeared brown and ready for reaping, in some of which people were busy at work, mowing shearing etc. Here both hay and corn is ready for housing the day after it is cut if the weather is fine which at this time was the case, an elderly person on the steam boat informed me that he did not recollect vegitation ever being in a more thriving state than at this season, the country having been favoured with seasonable and refreshing shower of rain with warm sun which caused the growth of vegitation to be abundant. At half past 4 o'clock we passed Pennsbury the spot where William Penn had his mansion house, it is a most beautiful and level situation. Here it was where he recieved his visitors in state, having a Hall for hearing and receiving petitions in and other state matters, the Indians visited him at this house. Nothing now remains of it saving the ruins and part of the fire place and chimney standing up perhaps 6 or 8 feet. He speaks of this place in his works - it is about 29 miles up the Delaware from Philadelphia - at 5 o'clock passed white hill and Bordan Tower, at which place is the country seat of Joseph Bonaparte, it is 3 or 4 miles above Pennsbury on the opposite side of the river. It appears a substantial and genteel house nearly surrounded with wood fronting the river, yet a pleasant and retired situation. We arrived at the hotel at Trenton a little after six in the evening, the weather being very fine I took a walk into a field where some people were at work taking up wheat and rye, it was fine and ripe. I assisted them to bind a sheaf or two - they did their work as I thought in a very loose manner. I was informed that they raked the field after being thus taken up, which I thought was very necessary. The corn in this country if pretty fine weather will be cut in one day and housed the next, the hay likewise, such is the power of the sun and the dryness of the air when the weather is favourable, which in summer is mostly clear and fine.

4th day the 16th

At 6 o'clock started in the stage from Trenton, the morning beautifully fine and pleasant, reached Prinston by 8 o'clock 11 miles, where we took breakfast and proceeded in the stage to New Brunswick where the steam boat from New York met us. After exchanging passengers and luggage we set forwards down the Rariton river, the afternoon being particularly serene and pleasant, the captain steered the boat outside the land down towards Sandyhook where vessels come in from Europe, here we had a view once more of the sea, the light house, Long Island and the highlands, all which was very pleasant to us, having been 6 weeks gone from this part. At about half past 4 o'clock we passed the narrows, having Fort Richmond on the left and Fort Diamond on our right, these are two powerful and commanding fortifications, the former especially, which stands on a very high hill. The sea is so narrow in this part that they could easily fire a cannon ball from land to land, so in this place an enimy would not be able to pass on any account. The next place 'is' about 2 or 3 miles is a large castle and battery. We percieved the guns, they appeared immensely large and frightfull. So we got safe once more to New York to our former lodgings in Broad Way at Widow Jane Saidlers - where we met with friend W.H. of Sheffield who also came from England in 4th month last a few days before us. About 6 o'clock in the evening after getting our luggage etc. a little sided I went to P&G's where I found letters from our homes by two seperate ships informing us of our own families being well at the date of 5th month 17th, for which account I believe we were both very thankful - they also informed us of the decease of several of our friends.

7th month, 5th day the 17th

Today employed in writing for the business as likewise in answering letters received from home yesterday, ship called the Draper being about to sail for Liverpool - the weather fine, clear and hot.

6th day the 18th

Attended on some little matters in the business with a walk in the evening. Today a south wind and oppressively hot - thermometer near 90'.

7th day the 19th

Being a very wet day both J.F. and myself stoped in house and wrote with some other little matters in which we were engaged.

1st day the 20th

Attended Liberty Street meeting in the morning and Pearl Street in the afternoon - the latter was a very hot and oppressive time, the evening being wet with thunder.

2nd day morning 21st

This morning a northerly wind and more cool. Account of arrivals at Boston from Liverpool reached us this morning informing us of the ship Triton going from Boston in 5th month last for Liverpool making her passage in 26 days, also the Courier from same place to Liverpool in 20 days. Both these vessels took us letters for our families - so that this was to us pleasing information.

3rd day 22nd

Being a rough wet and thundery day J.F. and myself stopped pretty much in house and wrote in the business account.

4th day 23rd

This morning fine clear and more pleasant after the lightening and thunder. In the forenoon I attended on change and observed eight different auction sales all going on at one and the same time, several of them in the open street, and so near together that where I stood I could hear what the Auctioneers said. The sales consisted of unmanufactured tobacco, indigo in skin, pepper, port wine, guns and spyglass, crates of pots, bales of hemp twine, chests of tea, casks of molasses or treacle with a variety of hardware. Sales of this sort are held every day, tho I did not recollect seeing so many so near together as on this day. The Auctioneers appeared particularly busy, I observed the leaf tobacco in hogsheads sold at 5 cents a lb. sterling 2 1/2 and other goods sold in proportion, very low.

5th day the 24th

This morning at 6 o'clock we packed up our things and took stage in company with James Sanderson on our way to Boston and in the day passed through the following small towns viz; Arlum, next West farms where resides Thomas Walker brother to Robert Walker of Darley in Yorkshire, as also Thomas Wright formerly of Sheffield, next passed through Sawpit, Norves, Saugastruck, Fairfield, Stradford, Milford and so to New Haven where we arrived about 9 o'clock having travelled the distance of 90 miles. The day being rather cloudy and cool was very pleasant. The farmers appeared busy in getting in the wheat which was generally ripe, the country from New York to New Haven is with respect to soil rather rocky and poor pretty much overgrown with wood - large fields of Indian corn grew with luxuriance all along this route, but the main product seems to be the apple orchards. These we observed almost in a continual wood and uncommonly loaded with fruit. The crop indeed was abundant beyond what we ever saw.

6th day the 25th

Having lodged at Newhaven at the Butlers Inn, we again took to the stage. As this town is noticed in my memorandums heretofore, I omit saying anything more about it now. We started at about 9 o'clock passing through a beautifull country more rich in soil than any I had before observed since arriving in this country. The corn fields and meadows with the scenary of the country being more broken with hill and dale rendered a truly delightful prospect. On our way we passed through Merridon, Berlin and so on to Hartford in the State of Konnecticut what is stiled the land of steady habits. The town of Hartford is built partly on the Konnecticut river in a very clean situation tho not large. Large brigs and schooners can lay to the wharfs - cod fishing seems to be a part of employment in the sloops, which go to the Newfoundland Banks and return with valuable cargoes of fish. Hartford is the Metropolis or chief town of the State of Connecticut and the seat of government and about 34 miles from Newhaven which was all the distance we travelled on this day, a poor days work.

7th day the 26th

Having made so little out on our journey yesterday we now thought of mending the matter and this morning about 1/2 past 5 o'clock we embarked ourselves and luggage in the mail stage, the morning fine and cool. For a few miles on our road from Hartford the land was rich and luxuriant. Indian corn, Tobacco, Wheat, rye and other produce grew in perfection. We passed through Vernon, Tolland and Stafford. At the last is a mineral spring and a bath which is frequented in the summer season by the citizens, resorting to this bath for recreation etc. The country in these parts is romantic. Rocky and barren much overgrown with wood which together with the salutory effects of the water draws company to behold the change from level and fertile fields to high hills and barren mountains. We next reached Storbridge to dine - a very clean and pleasant village, then to Charleton and Leicester. At the latter J.F. and myself alighted out of the stage and for 3 or 4 minutes went to look at a carding mill on a small scale they had one scribbler and one carder. Very neat little single engines, one large cylinder only. they appeared to do their work very well. They were carding white wool as we believed for the neighbouring farmers who would spin the same with one spindle on a home wheel for stocking yarn as also yarn to get wove into linen warp making a kind what may be called home made cassimere which seemed common in these thinly inhabited places. One may observe in passing along now and then a loom of this sort at a little wood house by the road side which is employed in this way. We now began to leave the mountains and a more cultivated and rich country presented itself to us, about 5 o'clock in the evening we reached the town of Worcester, a most beautiful place something like Newhaven. These smaller towns in this country are very different to towns of a similar size in Yorkshire. We mostly find such town in England built of brick and with the different manufactories smooked or nearly black, but these in America are invariably built of wood and mostly on a large and level open green with the publick road over the same. The houses on each side are not usually built to touch each other but singly with a space between say one a general store, next a tavern, next a farm house and so on. The church house or rather in their own phrase, as they are all called meeting houses, be of what society they may these places of worship if only one in the town it is mostly built in the middle of the green or open level of the town, by itself unenclosed as the grave yards are mostly from a quarter to 1/2 a mile out of the town on some detatched eminence. These meeting houses are invariably with the dwelling houses built of wood and often high steeples white washed or painted. these white looking towns upon a large level green plot hath a very pleasing appearance. The stage drivers generally blow their horns on entering these towns, and spring over the green full gallop till they arrive at the post office or place of changing horses. The drivers are very dextrous and the horses fleet are nimble equal to any I ever saw in England, but the carriages are shabby and far beneath the English ones. Of the forgoing description is the town of Worcester. After exchanging horses we proceeded on our way again, the evening was very fine and added to the eligant scenary of the country. We were now got in to the state of Massechusetts, passing through Shrewsbury and to Farmingham to supper then started again being 9 o'clock and very moonlight we passed onward and arrived safe in Boston as the clock struck one in the morning having come all the way from New York through the country by land conveyance, a distance of 230 miles.

1st day the 27th

Getting late in the night we went to the exchange coffee house the watchman shewing us to our rooms, so we got to bed pretty directly. In the morning D. Barnum the master of the house and the servants seemed pleased to see us. D.B. took J.F. around the house and gave us choice of the different rooms at liberty, so we got accommodated with very light airy and convenient lodgings - more comfortable than any we had been in before since our ariving in America. This was our first quarter on landing from England on the 4th of 5th month last. Being no meeting of friends held in Boston we put our things to rights and read with a little walk out towards evening.

2nd day the 28th

Attended to different matters. The weather fine and clear.

3rd day the 29th

Spent much the same as yesterday, thermometer now 90.

4th day the 30th

Pretty well employed writing on the business account. Took a walk to the wharfs in the evening. Some rain having in the afternoon made it cooler and more pleasant. I observed it was quite low water the sea having retired, a body of water 10 or 12 feet leaving the vessels resting their sides in the bare mud and the bay also bare for a great extent. This seems curious that in 6 hours the water will again return and rise up the sides of the wharfs 8 or 20 feet or more when all the ships will float about and so it is. The evening was particularly still. I saw the flags of the ships of war hauled down with usual ceremony.

5th day the 31st

This morning the wind north the atmosphere clear and fine. My time taken up in writing for the business.

6th day 8th month 1st

Again wrote today in the business account.

7th day the 2nd

In the forenoon was employed as yesterday in writing. In the afternoon I went on board the ship Mary and Susan about to sail for Liverpool in

England and from the deck of which I could see the bay, islands and country surrounding as also the lighthouse. the weather was particularly clear and fine I had a very pleasant view of the vessels going out and entering he habour. I fixed my attention on a sail approaching nearly as far as I could percieve out at sea and having leisure I concluded to observe the arrival. The wind was brisk and fair for making the harbour, so in a short time I discovered my object to be a ship which drew nearer and nearer until about pistol shot from the wharf where I was standing and then backed sails and dropped her anchor. She proved to be a ship from the East Indies with merchandise and passengers, the latter I observed soon came on shore after a passage as I understood of near two months. This, though a common occurance yet no doubt it was interesting to those concerned.

1st day the 3rd

Being first day I stoped in house pretty much and read my bible. Here is no meeting of friends held Boston, yet I felt very comfortable and quiet alone.

2nd day the 4th

At about 6 o'clock this morning I was rapped up by John Lees a friend who had come from England about 6 years ago and settled in this state, who I was glad to see, having not had the opportunity before since my arrival in America. I believe the meeting on both sides was very agreeable, he being particularly desirous of my going to his house, so with J. Fisher's concent I started off with him in his carriage about 3 o'clock in the afternoon and passing through a pleasant country in agreeable conversation much concerning former event and circumstances, we arrived at his house about 12 o'clock. We had a pleasant ride the weather being warm and fine, distance from Boston 40 miles.

3rd day the 5th

A fine morning not over hot. I rose early, my friends situation is in a level fertile valley in the country of Worcester about 7 miles from said town. He owns a share in a mill near to his residence upon a copious stream and an advantageous fall. This mill is employed in spinning cotton as also in grinding corn and sawing timber. The cotton is a stout strong yarn for sewing thread with some that he dyes and makes into small striped cloth called the American domestic calico which is strong and serviceable. After going through the mill we next walked along his farm consisting of about 200 acres in the flat before mentioned. I observed it to be cultivated much like our Yorkshire land, with wheat, oats, barley, potatoes and an addition of Indian corn 8 or 9 feet high. His cows were rather of a small kind but his oxen used in the yoke were pretty large and strong. So having gone pretty much over his premises we dined and about 2 o'clock started in his gig towards Boston. On the road we came and after a pleasant ride, the weather being particularly fine, we arrived safe, he to his Inn and I to my lodging at the Exchange coffee house about 10 o'clock in the evening.

4th day the 6th

Fine morning, clear atmosphere and wind westerly. Had little employment this day. Towards evening took a walk with my friend J.Lees. we observed a vessel putting off from the wharf called the William of Liverpool bound to said port. She was a brig of a description not very desirable to go out in for safety being high out of the water. The wind being fair she got quickly under way after the crew had shook hands with their friends standing on the wharf. In an hour she would be quite out of sight of town. It is interesting to observe a scene of this sort, the sailors and passengers on board taking leave of their relations and friends perhaps never to meet again in this state of existance. Just as the ship puts off from land there is such hurry of uniting hands over the sides of the vessel while she is gently moving off, some can scarsely reach so as to touch fingers being in danger of falling into the water amidst the general cry of goodby, goodby and farewell boys, God bless you etc. etc.

5th day the 7th

Fine clear harvest weather. This morning I took leave of my friend John Lees with whom I had spent a little time very agreeably, he is now proposing to return home. Today I packed up our mattresses and other bedding which we used on our passage from England and as our prospect was to embark at New York I accordingly shipped said bedding to that port in hopes of soon having the satisfaction to use the same on our passage over the ocean homewards. In the afternoon the wind southerly and very close and hot.

6th day the 8th

Wind south and very close and oppressive, hot. Today being wet I stoped in house pretty much and read with some other little matters on the business which I attended to, in the evening took a little walk, but the weather still continuing warm and wet I took to the house again. J.F now fully concluded for us to finally leave Boston.

DIARY FOUR

8th month 7th day the 9th

Still close and hot. This morning we packed up our things in order to leave this place finally for the year 1817 and about 12 o'clock we start with a full mail stage load of passengers to the number of 10 persons in the inside. We got on pretty well except a few little breakages about the carriage and harness etc. which our driver had occasionally to stop and put to rights. On our way we passed through Farmingham where we dined, then passing along the country and over a curious constructed bridge near Worcester. It is rather through a deep pond or lake made a little more than even with the surface of the water by laying pieces of timber across each other in an horizontal manner and sinking them, in this way they had sunk wood to the depth of 60 ft below the surface of the water which if it has been a stage standing that height above ground it would appear alarming to have passed over in a coach and four without anything as a battlement or side which was the case with this. Yet we passed over with the greatest safety and arrived at Worcester about 8 o'clock, the ride had been very unpleasant as we were much crowded in the stage, the weather likewise was very close wet and hot, often changing horses and some of our passengers also stopping. We started again and arrived at Storbridge about 11 o'clock where we took supper changed our stage and horses and off again. The night was very dark and lonesome together with the hard and hilly road rendered the travelling very irksome, but with care we got well to Stafford Springs about half past 3 o'clock and changed our carriage and horses again, when in about an hour afterwards growing a little light the danger seemed now pretty much over, we most of us I believe fell asleep. Our company now being dwindled to four J.F. and myself, James Sanderson and another person a stranger to us, so about half past seven we arrived safe at the Exchange Coffee House at Hartford in the state of Connecticutt the place we had visited about two weeks before, for which reason shall observe nothing more particular about it here as it will be found mentioned in my memorandums on our former visit to said place. Distance from Boston to Hartford by this route about 100 miles.

1st day the 10th

Having travelled through the night and being first day morning we felt dirty and uncomfortable, but being pretty well as to health we set about shaving and cleaning ourselves after which I suppose we might appear rather more respectable. As no meeting of friends is settled in Hartford J.F. went to visit an acquaintance and I kept to my room pretty much, having not much inclination to be out. As the weather still continued very warm yet more dry in the evening J.F. concluded upon my going to Springfield by the first stage which started in the morning about 4 o'clock, accordingly at bedtime I arranged our luggage to be ready.

2nd day the 11th

At the time above mentioned I took leave of Hartford, the morning being dry and a great deal cooler so much so that I could bear my great coat on very comfortably. I left J.Fisher behind, he intended to follow me in a carriage with a friend in the evening. Our road led through the most fertile part of the country all along the banks of the Connecticut river, on a continual level plane. The soil appeared pretty rich rather of a loose sandy kind. Tobacco and Indian corn grew in great perfection as also apples, the wheat and other grain of that kind was entirely harvested in. The road was most pleasant of any I have travelled in America being very level and almost a continual green or grass plot with here and there a stragling farm house. The river on our left had also a very pleasing appearance, something like the Delaware about Pennsbury. About 7 o'clock arrived at Endfield a small white town on the green under cover of large elm and other trees - here we took breakfast consisting of fried stakes, potatoes, egs, cheese and coffee the regular Yankee custom. Starting from hence and passing onwards through scenary as in our first drive, we arrived at Springfield about nine o'clock, distance from Hartford about 26 miles through a country that I thought was the best land (in continuation) as also the best managed of any I had before seen in the United States. J.Fisher as proposed arrived in the evening. We were lodged at J.Bennetts Tavern, a comfortable clean country house.

3rd day the 12th

A very heavy rain fell during the whole of the night and continued till near noon on this day, which discouraged the farmers those of them who had got any of the remains of their rye out. The town of Springfield is of a sort with the rest of ye American small settlements a very clean and sweet whitewashed situation, rather more scattered than some, its population is computed at about twenty eight hundred mostly farmers with a few store keepers and other domestic tradespeople. The town itself is built pretty much of wood upon the banks of the Connecticut river, 26 miles from Hartford in the state of Massachusetts. At this place is an excellent stream and an advantageous fall, upon which is the great state government manufactory for arms such as guns, swords, pistols etc. I was informed that 250 men are regularly employed in this way who are calculated to make 1000 stand of arms per month which are stood in a large arsenal on the premises. This appears singular and also serious, that in a country that is professing to avoid wars and live at peace with all men should still be making of so many instruments of death intended for the sole purpose of killing and destroying beings possessing faculty and soul like themselves (but enough of this here). About this part are great numbers of tree frogs which lodge in the trees and at the dusk of the evening make a very great chirping noise something like the English sparrow but much louder being more numerous especially at Hartford. I observed that in the country places in the New England states the farmer men and boys appeared to generally go without shoes or stockings, for instance, as we passed along in the stage it would be no unusual thing to meet a group of labourers going to work in the fields and perhaps all of them without shoes or stockings. I presume that this practice is not kept to in winter as the weather is at times very inclement. The weather in the afternoon of the day continuing wet and warm I did not go very far from my lodging, saving to a small paper mill at which I did not observe anything very particular. At bedtime J.F. concluded I should leave Springfield and take the stage for Northampton he following with a friend in a gig. I almost felt regret at leaving John Bennetts our boarding house, the family and accommodations were so much more agreeable than any we had before met with, having good beds and but little company great attention was payed us by the whole family which altogether rendered our short stay at the town of Springfield very comfortable.

4th day the 13th

At 7 o'clock packed up and prepared for taking leave of Springfield and at 10 started in the coach or stage for Northampton passing along the country pretty near to the Connecticut river as before. A few miles from Springfield the stage stopped to allow the passengers the opportunity of looking at a pair of very large oxen brought up and feeding by a farmer ajoining to the turnpike road. They were uncommonly large exeeding any I ever saw in England; the larger especially, I could just reach to his huggan with my chin; he did not appear to be particularly fat but huge in bone and a great length, his weight exceeded one and a half tons, about 6 years old. Leaving here we passed on and was obliged to go over the Hadly mountains in consequence of the late rains having drove out the river beyond its regular bounds into the fields and road, the new route led us a great way about, over a very steep mountain so much so that the passengers were glad to get out and walk and with care reached Hadly where the stage left me, 3 miles short of Nothampton. I here dined and the tavern keeper undertook to convey me and the luggage in a little waggon (a kind of carriage very common in the state of Massachusets) to my destined place, so we embarked ourselves in this machine crossing through the water in the road up to the horses belly but our weight kept the waggon on its wheels and we got pretty well to the side of the river, which we had to cross in a flat bottomed boat called a scone - the water was so far out into the fields that it was difficult to get the horse and carriage shipped; having to put both down a brink side, the horse being I supposed used to such kind of work as he glided down very gently into the boat to my astonishment and the boatmen lifted in the waggon, so being now on board along with 3 other horses, several men and two waggons in a flat open boat within about 6 inches of the water, we put off into the stream. the river was very high and running pretty rapidly, say 6 knots an hour and great logs of timber floating as wreck on all sides. the situation looked a little precarious especially had the horses become unruly, but favourably for us they stood still as a stock and our ferryman being dextrous we got well over for which I felt thankfull and in a few minutes arrived at Levi Limans in Northampton about 4 o'clock. While crossing the river I thought I had never felt the sun shine hotter, it fairly pinched me through my cloths in such a manner that I scarcely knew where to put myself, and afterwards I was attacked with a violent headake, but on laying down a little and taking a cup of strong tea I recovered to my great satisfaction. Northampton is a town or village of the American description clean whitewashed on an open flat green (not large). About 7 o'clock J.Fisher arrived as expected and it was agreed if the stage got up, to proceed on towards Albany the regular time about 4 o'clock in the morning. I may first notice that our quarters at Levi Limans Northampton was for a few hours we stopped pretty comfortable except for being a little annoyed with what may be styled an American Ball or play (a black man scraping a fiddle in an ajoining room and performing ventriloquism) accompanied with laughter in roars usual at these amusements.

5th day the 14th

At about 4 o'clock started in the mail stage as expected, drove to Chesterfield 14 miles to breakfast, then set forward through a mountainous and romantick country but generally better soil and a higher state of cultivation than on the shores of New England states. In this route we passed through several small towns and villages viz: Perue, Hensley, Pittsfield, at the last is a large barracks where the British Prisoners of War were kept during the last conflict to the number of two thousand, next through Lebanon and Canaan, the country is very fine and the soil good in this district. Very large cedar timber and oak grows to perfection in this part, here is a small settlement of people residing in this neighbourhood who call themselves shaken quakers. We were informed that they resembled friends in some moral matters but their mode of worship differed very much, they being singular in some other delicate opinions which I omit on said account, yet understand they are an orderly people and very ingenious and neat in their manner of living. They live in large families of 80 persons in one house and have a common stock. They have arrived to great perfection in gardening and derive great proffit from the sale of garden seeds. We dined at an Inn near Nassau and afterwards passed through said village, all the towns mentioned in this days travel are much same as others of a description peculiar to the United States of America particulars of which may be found in different parts of my former memorandums. Towards evening we passed by a large cantonement where was an army stationed during the latter part of the late war with England, so after a ride this day from Northampton of about 74 miles we arrived at 1/2 past 7 o'clock on the banks of the river Hudson mostly called the North River and in a short time we were ferried over, coach and horses to the opposite shore where stands the City of Albany. The night was dark wet and hot and in consequence of so much company being on the move to and from the Saratoga watering place, we found but uncomfortable lodgings, our beds consisted of some kind of frame something like a winterhedge* that folded up, and when opened it formed a hammock; on this was laid a small bed, of an ordinary sort (our sheets) both J.F. and myself believed were so damp as by no means fit to sleep in, so we took them off and made up our couch with greatcoats and other cloths as well as we could and passed the night very uncomfortably.

*A winterhedge is the Yorkshire name for a clothes-horse, a wooden frame upon which clothes etc. were dried.

6th day the 15th

The city or town of Albany is built pretty much of brick especially the new part on the west side of the river Hudson it is not a place of any very large extent, the inhabitants are computed at about 15,000, yet it is the capital of the State of New York and also the seat of the government. The general courts and other publick business is held and transacted at this place. It is about 164 miles by water from last mentioned city viz New York. (I may just observe here that the hilly parts of the country from Springfield to Albany especially about Perue, is poor and backward, their oats and wheat are cut green and very little of their hay got in full as late in season; as in different parts of Yorkshire in England. (We passed this part on the 14th of 8th month)

The weather today 8/15 was very warm and close, the morning part in particular which was very discouraging to the farmers, those of them who had grain out, as the late rain with the succeeding close warm air would cause the corn to grow very quick. In the evening more clear and dry. J.F. and myself took a walk round the city. we observed many very substantial and hansome buildings. Albany may be considered the largest inland town of any in the United States, the river is large and navigable for vessels of 200 tons berthen, yet small craft come up here such as one mast sloops, and lesser boats. We did not see a two mast vessel of any sort, not even a schooner, the river being so serpentine that the navigation up the same and against the stream is very tedious, even with a fair wind, so much for Albany.

7th day the 16th

This morning we arose early packed up our things and about 9 o'clock we set forward in the steam boat Richmond from Albany down the Hudson on our way to New York. The passengers at the time appointed for the boat to start flocked on board in crowds, something like the breaking up of a place of worship. 13 carriages stood about the boat unloading luggage and passengers besides common carts and porters, such is the concourse of people travelling to and from the springs at this time of the year from the southerly parts of the States. The fair from Albany to New York including all eatings, the distance of 164 miles is 8 dollars or sterling 36/-. I counted 80 persons at dinner table say 8 dollars each is 640 dollars, sterling £144. The captain informed me he had not more company than usual, four of these trips performed in a week leaves a hansome sum at the years end. At 12 o'clock reached the town of Hudson 30 miles from Albany on the banks of the river from whence it derives its name i.e. the river Hudson or North river. The town is rather small and built upon high rocky ground. Larger shipping come to this place than those which go to Albany being better to get to. On the opposite shore is the small town of Athens as also the Catskill mountains, towering their lofty heads upwards three thousand feet above the level of the river. These hills have a very curious appearance their dark summits are to be seen above the light coloured clouds which may be percieved gliding gently on the valley below. This scenary exceeded anything I ever saw in England. It is mentioned by Robert Sutcliffe in his account of this part of America. The steam boats that navigate this river are the first rate of this class of vessels; the proprietors have obtained the sole right to its navigation by a grant from the government for 20 years to come, which in that time will put money into their hands to an amazing amount. At 6 o'clock put passengers ashore at Ploughkeepsie and at 8 o'clock repeated the same at Newburgh. The daylight was now gone yet being a fine evening with a new moon which was very acceptable we got alongside what is called the highland mentioned by Robert Sutcliffe. The river is much contracted by these amazing high hills which stand almost perpendicular out of the water to the height of 1400 feet. The current of wind blew through this channel like unto a gale whilst in the open river it was almost a perfect calm. To a stranger they appear awefully grand, so after observing the scenary till near eleven o'clock, - we concluded to try our berths. With about 60 persons in the same room and contrary to our expectations we both slept a few hours I believe soundly till near 4 o'clock when we rose and went on deck being then about the day break and being in sight of New York. Shortley afterwards landed and went to our former lodgings at Jane Saidlers in Broadway having a very pleasant sail down the large river Hudson which is in many parts from one to two miles over (say in several places near 3 miles from shore to shore) This trip was performed 164 miles in about 22 hours, by far quicker and easier than by stage and with a few exceptions much more safe.

This picture shows a typical North River Steamboat Co. ship of the type travelled on by John Adamson along the Hudson river and described in his diaries. (Reproduced by courtesy of the Peabody Museum of Salem)

1st day the 17th

After our arrival at our lodgings we cleaned for the day and was ready for breakfast when the bell rung, previous to which I went to Robert Pearsalls to enquire for our letters and to great satisfaction found the same from our families in England as late as the 26th of 6th month leaving at that time our relations and friends well. This is one of the most agreeable occurrances that a person from home in a foriegn country can be gratified with viz. that of recieving letters from their friends at home. Both J.F. and myself attended meeting at Liberty Street, our friend Stephen Grelett handed a few words in great affection. Today pretty warm yet mostly dry.

2nd day the 18th

Today very hot, thermometer at 84 by 10 o'clock in the morning. Was pretty well employed for the business, also replied to the letters received yesterday from home and sent same by the brig Favourite.

3rd day the 19th

This morning packed up our things again and took steam boat for Philadelphia. Started at 7 o'clock passing up the Rariton river as in our first journey to that place, and so on to Trenton to lodge.

4th day the 20th

At 6 o'clock embarked on the steam boat on the River Delaware from Trenton; a friend being the commander of said vessel. The morning was fine and hot and the scenary on each side most beautiful, as mentioned in my memorandums when last up this river. About half after eleven o'clock we once more landed at the city of Philadelphia and as cousin John Sharp was now got married and a home keeper, he came for me to the steam boat after hearing of our arrival and took me to his house where both he and his wife payed me great attention. J.Fisher went to stay a few days at Edward Wilsons, so we were both now lodging with our friends for the few days we had in prospect of spending at Philadelphia.

5th day the 21st

Today attended friends meeting at Arch Street and afterwards walked through the market where I observed fruit in abundance such as peaches which sold at 50 cts a strike that is 2/3d sterling. Soft sun fruit was also very plentiful viz cucumbers, squashes, water melons, tomatus, mush melon or whatever is more generally known by nutmeg and boiled Indian corn which the coloured women carry about the streets in small kits calling hot corn, hot corn, this seems to be a favourite dish. They are sold at a cent an ear. The water melons are very large say from 10lb to 60lb and may be bought for as many cents and other fruits in proportion. Shambles meat sold this day at about say mutton or lamb 7 cts. or 3 1/4d sterling, veal 10 cts and beef the same, 5 1/2d sterling. Butter very good 37 1/2 cts a lb. sterling 20d eggs a cent each, flour about 11 dollars a barrel of 196lb. 3/3d. per stone English.

6th day the 22nd

This morning more agreeably cool than had been for some weeks past, for which I felt very thankful as I had of late been much overset with the heat of the weather. I attended on some little matters in the business and accompanied cousin John Sharp to see a friends family in the evening.

7th day the 23rd

Recipe for restoring apple trees which have by age become so weak as to only produce small apples; strip the bark from the ground as high as 10 feet on the 4th day of the 7th month, taking care not to let anything touch the trees for two months afterwards, when a new thin bark will replace the old and the next year the fruit will be twice as large and more abundant and not taste of the tree as before. This is only to be done with trees which, although old are not decayed in their trunks.* This morning I accompanied John Moor and John Hoyle Jnr to visit the religious German emigrants lately arrived in this city, and for a short time friends had accomodated these people 250 including men, women and children with part of a large house intended for an institution for sick persons, situate at Bush hills. They appeared glad to see us. J.Moor, a young man from near London our companion could speak French, as also could one of these people, so we conversed for some time pretty agreeably. I found they had left their country pretty much on account of being persecuted for their religious principals which are very much similar to those of friends, they seemed very clean and serious. I learnt that several of them had come through Permont in 3rd month last. Their view is to retire to the back parts of the country and there cultivate for themselves. Their general appearance was singular, very different from the English both in person and dress, say in stature rather short and thick, the head rather large with round forehead and long hare, yet their whole deportment was greatly superior to the other emigrants from the same country, being far more clean and orderly. The womens petticoats very short and full with their pace slow. Friends interest themselves a good deal in their account and have formed a committee to assist and further their prospects. In the evening I bathed in the Delaware which was very cooling and pleasant.

* *According to professional gardeners such treatment would surely kill any apple tree ! In view of the suggested date (Independence Day), was someone having a quiet joke at the expense of the diarist ?*

1st day the 24th

In the night lightening and rain the wind changing from due south to north by west. The climate was now quite changed likewise becoming much more cool for which I felt thankful having been for some weeks back oppressive hot so that a person could hardly sleep with the sheet cover only, but now able to lay comfortably under both blanket and counterpane such the transition from heat to cold. Today attended meeting in 12th Street in the morning and Green Street in the afternoon, which completed my visit to each one of the five different meetings held in the city viz. Pine Street, Arch Street, Fourth Street or North meeting, Twelfth Street and the last Green Street. Those of this day were to my satisfaction. In the afternoon at Green Street friends were favoured with about 20 of the religious German imigrants; those mostly women dressed in their own form in very short petticoats without anything as a gown, only a kind of waistcoat and apron with some sort of little coloured cap tied over the head and under the chin, yet all particularly clean and serious. During the sitting a man friend felt strongly engaged to say something to them by interpreter but no-one in the meeting could be procured to perform the office altho several present could speak the German language, this was a great trial to the friend who was obliged to give up the task for that time, yet hopes were entertained of a future opportunity and a propper arrangement at some time, for an interpreter. One friend had a good deal to deliver in testimony in the meeting yet all in English, so that the poor Germans could reap no benefit from it. At the breaking up of the assembly I observed the strangers to arrange themselves in a kind of procession two and two; so walking seriously away. This scene was to me truly affecting. No matter what colour, language, shape of person or people, they that fear god and work rightiousness are accepted of Him.

2nd day the 25th

Fine cool English weather that I enjoyed as such, being able to walk about without sweating to such a degree as was the case a few days back. Attending on different little matters during the day.

3rd day the 26th

Our prospect for embarking for England now appeared to increase and I this day began to make some little preparations on that account. The weather continued fine and more cool.

4th day the 27th

Attended on different business that fell out. I observed with curiosity as one of the German women with a child in her hand was walking along the street a genteel person stopped and got into conversation with them (the poor German and her child) and while I looked on, the lady presented the child with a piece of siver called a 5d. bit. The mother directed the child to observe its manners, whereupon it orderly kissed the back of the hand of its kind benefactress. I supposed this to be in lieu of our English bow and thank you.

5th day the 28th

This morning packed up our things and at one o'clock started leaving the city of Philadelphia finally for 1817. We embarked on board the steam boat taking the same route as before up the Delaware. The tide being in our favour we got on pretty well and arrived at the usual quarters at Trenton about 6 o'clock in the evening.

6th day the 29th

Left our friend and companion E.Wilson at Trenton he returning by steam boat to Philadelphia and we on the stage overland towards New Brunswick which place we reached about 11 o'clock in the forenoon of this day. About 12 o'clock the steam boat Olive Branch from New York arrived and after the passengers from that place had cleared off we in return embarked. The weather being rather cool and the passengers fewer in number made it more agreeable travelling than when as about 5 weeks back the weather was over setting hot and the vessel crowded with people. Being a fine afternoon the captain took the boat past Sandy Hook and about 6 o'clock in the evening we landed at the city of New York. I may notice here that on the steam boats arriving, a great number of poor labouring coloured people attend as porters to convey the passengers and baggage to where they be going. These men would almost frighten any stranger as when the vessel comes near enough the wharf they all rush on board like a pirate's crew boarding a merchant man. Today I observed this uncultivated set of men awaiting for us landing, whereupon I put our luggage to itself intending to wait until the hurry was a little over, and as I expected as soon as we came within a leap of the shore, the black porters rushed on board in their usual manner and being but few passengers and but little baggage they got to differing about who was to carry it, and presently to fighting which caused a great uproar on board, with the men knocking about and the captain and mate pushing them on shore. It was all even I could do to keep myself on my feet and my portmanteaus from being tumbled overboard. After the captain and mate or steward had succeeded in clearing the deck they kept up the tumult on shore, some fighting and others looking, whilst a few more crafty than the rest, got all the baggage to carry and set off with it. So in this I saw the old proverb verifyed (that while two fight a third runs away with the bone.) Got well to our usual quarters at 36 Jane Saidlers.

7th day the 30th

This morning set about preparing for our passage home by the ship Amity in earnest, getting our bedding etc. aired and fit to go on board to sleep in, also attended on sundry things on the business account, the weather now becoming warm again.

1st day the 31st

Attended Liberty Street meeting, both fore and afternoon sittings to my great satisfaction and comfort. During the interval and in the evening I copied for J.Fisher the whole of the London Yearly Meeting Epistle of the 5th month inclusive from the 25th to the 30th of the present year 1817.

2nd day 9th month 1st

This morning we packed up our things and got the same on board the ship Amity which was no pleasant piece of work as it looked like something of setting our faces homeward once again. In the evening I received several letters from my wife and friends at home which was truly acceptable and being so near about to return towards our native land. These letters bore date of 7th month 8th and 10th then leaving our families and friends well. A great satisfaction to a person in a foriegn country.

3rd day the 2nd

Spent the day pretty much in taking leave of our American friends in New York and settling off our concerns. At night we went on board to make up our births and put our luggage to rights. Also slept on board for the first time and for my own part, comfortably.

4th day the 3rd

Today was taken up with making appointments when to go on board, as also to get all the passengers together which was as is generally the case the day appointed for embarking, one being gone this way and another the other way to take leave of their friends etc. etc. However, the ship got under way and anchored in the north river at the contrary side of the city. J.F. and myself with many other passengers got on board to sleep.

5th day the 4th of 9th month 1817

Soon after daylight this morning the Captain and the remaining passengers came on board after which the Pilot put the ship in motion being about half past seven o'clock and a fine morning - yet the wind rather against us blowing southerly, but being ebb tide we got up to the narrows by 12 o'clock and then let go the anchor waiting for the return of the tide in our favour. Our crew consisted of Captain John Stanton and two maits, two stewards, one cabin boy, eleven seamen, fourteen cabin passengers (two of whom were women, two children, two steerage passengers and a coloured man cook, in all 35 persons. The ship was quite full both of lading and passengers, the latter was none of them known to me except J.F. and John Hustler of Rawdon near Leeds. One thing I may notice which seemed very domestick, that was the women sewing and the children prattling and singing away just as if on shore, even so, at the return of the tide the wind being ahead our pilot and captain judged it most prudent to lay where we were till morning. In the evening some of our passengers who had gone ashore in the afternoon came aboard and while alongside of the ship a rope was thrown out to them to hold on by as the tide was running out rapidly, and just as the rope was going over it accidentally struck against a passenger on deck, checked hold of his watch chain and pulled the watch and all overboard into the sea. This was a mortifying disappointment, the person said it cost him fifteen guineas, was the same less or more, it was lost to him for ever. The water in this place may be 20 feet deep or more. This disappointment I was an eyewitness to, as I saw the watch plop into the water like a small fish. The night was very hot, with lightening.

6th day the 5th

About 6 o'clock this morning the wind and tide favourable our ship got under sail gliding gently through the narrows towards the lighthouse at Sandy Hook which we passed about 11 o'clock when the tide set up against us and we again dropped the anchor. In the afternoon left the Hook and with a fine breeze of southerly wind got out to sea. The pilot left us about 4 o'clock. Several of the passengers sent letters by him to their friends but for my own part I had no-one particular to send to; mine being in the country to which we were now steering. In the evening a brisk wind with a good deal of motion - many of our company became very sick, myself for one.

7th day the 6th

After a good night for sailing the wind got round to North by West and more cool yet I continued very unwell, I think as much so as in our passage from England and in the evening came a thick fog with a little rain.

1st day the 7th

The wind got this morning to north east and rather strong the ship being close to the wind caused a good deal of motion, myself and most of the passengers were in the fore part very sick. This is a curious scene to one that is quite well, to observe 10 or 12 persons all throwing up over the side of the vessel at one and the same time. Towards the evening we several of us recovered very finely so as to walk about again which was a favour although the motion of the vessel continued rather heavy, yet I was so far recovered as to be able to write this days memorandum, having a box lid for my writing desk. At 1/2 past 6 o'clock we discovered a brig to windward of us under her main and top sails but as our ship in addition carried top gallants we gained on her very fast though she appeared to be steering the same course as ourselves. Now a headwind and rough sea.

2nd day the 8th

Still a head wind with heavy sea and the motion violent. Our company continued to be very sickly especially the two females. The one in particular who was as is called deadly sick. Our Captain, J.Stanton greatly to his credit, observing this morning the poor womans condition, kindly brought her up on deck and afterwards fetched up her bed and bedding spreading the same in the open air and gently handing the sickly creature to lay down thereon in a most kind and affectionate manner, straightening her cloths and covering her in the strictest and most delicate way possible for the situation, and also with the men constructed a shade with a sail so as to prevent the hot sun beating upon her as well as the rest of the sick company. We were now in the gulf stream which I attributed as being cause of our oversetting sickness, the air and the sea being warm and full of vapour, even the poor goat became here so sick as to lose her milk and I noticed the sagacious creature smelling about the sick womans bed and afterwards as if with a degree of fellow feeling lay down at her feet. This female appeared to be a very respectable person, a single woman going to some part of the West of England, she was particularly neat in dress as also very modest in her carriage, one that had a regard to reading her Bible. In the afternoon light wind and not so hot; in the night a calm which was acceptable as it gave us an opportunity for a good sleep, which seemed to cure the whole company as on 3rd day the 9th in the morning we rose all well. The weather was particularly fine and the sea smooth our ship this morning steered nearly her course at about 3 knots an hour - in the afternoon the wind became contrary and continued so the whole of the night.

4th day the 10th

A fine pleasant morning but still a head wind, as yet we had been favoured with very little fair sailing. In the afternoon we were diverted in observing a shoal of rudder fish which almost constantly follow the rudder of the ship. They are about the size of a small herring and keep dodging about the rudder as long as the vessel is cutting its way through the water, in the same manner as we see a swarm of flies bussing about a horses ears on a warm day in summer. Very fine, with almost a calm the whole of the day.

5th day the 11th

New moon, with a change of wind, rather brisk from the southward. This day commenced with good sailing at from 7 to 8 knots in our direct course, the weather now very hot, thermometer at 80 upwards in the shade, brisk wind all this day and good sailing.

6th day the 12th

The last night, fine wind but being southerly it was very close and hot, in the forenoon still continued favourable for sailing. At 12 0'clock the Captain and mate took an observation and found we had gone over 4 degrees longitude in the last 24 hours; being in our course homewards 184 miles in one day. The weather was now settled and fine, the captain got the altitude so far, every day, and the men continued to make ropes and repair the rigging much same as in our passage out in the Liverpool Packet to Boston. Our ships company were now all recovered from sickness and employed themselves with reading, writing etc. all pretty comfortable for the situation. This day closed with good sailing and fine pleasant weather.

7th day the 13th

Again favoured by a brisk fair wind this morning getting along from 9 to 10 knots an hour in direct course. We began to approach the great fishing banks of Newfoundland. The sea fowl and flying fish now made their appearance. In the afternoon still brisk wind and rather squally. At night high sea with much lightening, the motion violent all which continued till morning.

1st day the 14th

A continuation of rough water and highish wind, our studing sails, spanker and main royals had been taken in during the night and whilst I was contemplating that the captain would be laying the ship too, to my astonishment I heard him give the order to hoist up the spanker on aft sheet, miszen stay sail, royal and studding sails after which the vessel cut through the rough water near 10 knots an hour, the wind at same time blowing what is called fair, say from south west upon our starboard quarter and pretty fresh. So far as I could learn from my own observation as also by information from others, our Commander Captain

John Stanton was very much master of his business, he informed me himself that for the last forty years he had performed two or three voyages a year to England and other parts of Europe, which long course of experience undoubtedly gives him great confidence in his person. Rather above the middle stature, and portly; yet diligent and careful, still fulfilling a seaman's duty by keeping his regular watch in his turn in the night with the first and second mate, in the daytime and in dangerous sailing is ever on the look out, he appears of a settled undaunted spirit independant and preserving, giving his orders in a sharp and strong tone of voice which are obeyed with the greatest of dexterity and respect both by the officers and men. I observed him this morning (with a great degree of pleasure) give to the sailors in the forecastle 3 new bibles and two tracts of the account of the Marine Bible Society in New York, at the same time requesting that they might be read frequently and kept clean. This struck me as coming from a feeling mind, yet I have heard him at times let out unguarded words - still who of us are without faults. Our ship called the Amity of New York was built in 1815 under Capt.J.Stanton's immediate inspection, a very fine and firm fast sailing vessel far superior to any I had before known so particularly, being very dry, buoyant and riding the rough wave more easily than what I had before witnessed - so much for Captain and ship. Our men this morning broached the fifth hogshead of water. This precious liquid is narrowly watched both by Captain and mates, and when they see anyone extravegant they will sometimes remind such of the great impropriety of their conduct. First day noon on the banks of Newfoundland rain and foggy unpleasant weather. By the calculations of today we appeared to have got over near 200 miles of longitude during the last twenty four hours. Our first mate kept the Log Book, making up the ships reckoning each day after taking the altitude of the sun at 12 o'clock at noon. The rules observed amongst the sailors and others on board were very much the same as on the ship Liverpool packet, and I understood that the American Merchant men had pretty much similar rules throughout the trade. About 4 o'clock the wind got round to north and east squally with heavy rain, and in the evening and night got to a gale. About midnight I went on deck and found the ship almost stripped of her sails and labouring very much, the sea ran very high and the night dark, the light coloured soaring waves had a phosphorous appearance resembling light coloured fire. This scenary was awefully grand and I thought exceeded anything we had seen in our passage out, yet amongst all this the captain did not bring the ship too.

2nd day the 15th

This morning the wind and sea much the same as last night and nearly ahead of us , about 11 o'clock I observed the thermometer had fallen near 20 degrees it now standing at 62 in the shade on deck and 24 hours before had regularly stood at 80, but as we were now out of the American waters and in the British seas our climate became so much changed. I now laid by the thin tammy waistcoat for the thick woollen one, and in addition to that both J.F. and myself wore our great coats. In the evening the weather cleared up a little and the wind somewhat abated though still blowing ahead of us from the north east in squalls.

3rd day the 16th

Yet a head wind but not quite so strong as last night, thermometer in the shade on deck at 66, yesterday at 62 - now in fine clear dark blue water as salt as salt itself. This morning our under steward lost the table cloth as carelessly shaking the same over the side of the vessel the sea then running pretty high it was soon out of sight. In the afternoon the wind rather lulled yet continued in the same quarter, fine and dry weather with new moon.

4th day the 17th

This morning the wind due east right ahead, our Captain put the ship on the other tack and steered to the northward, the cook this morning killed the third sheep and also the third pig. Our livestock of cattle on board at the commencement of the passage consisted of eight live sheep, eleven hogs, about ten dozen of ducks and fowls and a female goat which the steward milked twice a day. She gave about a gill of rich sweet milk at a time which was very convenient, it serving for the tea and far more preferable than preserved cream. This goat was a very domestick tame creature and almost everyone's pet, yet very mischievous; stealing the corn from the fowls, the cabbage and potatoes from the cook or apples - in short anything she could get hold of. She also shewed her inclination to prefer the mountain, as described by a writer. She would frequently be on the very top of the stuff piled in the long boat, or if anyone seemed about to correct her for pilfering she would instantly return to the highest place she could find about the vessel possible for her to get to. At 9 o'clock thermometer at 68, yesterday at 66. This day closed with highish head wind and but difficult sailing for us.

5th day the 18th

The wind a little more favourable yet the ship was not able to steer her course when close hauled nearer than about north east and laying upon her side as much so as the steap roof of a house. This is a very unpleasant position as it renders it impossible to walk on deck or even to lay in one's birth on the windward side, so as to be the least comfortable. At noon a brig appeared to windward of us and having the same fair soon dropped astern. In the evening the wind veered round to south as also the sea became more smooth that we now got to what is called free sailing on a fair wind - this favour seemed to put new life into our company as we had been beating against the wind and wave for 3 days ever since first day night the 14th. A stranger cannot conceive the pleasure there is in being favoured with a fair wind at sea after several days and nights of head winds and rough weather.

6th day the 19th

This morning south wind and smoothish water - good sailing in our direct course at eight knots and upwards an hour. Orders were now given to hoist the light sails viz, the main royals, flying gib and stay sails which was a pleasant piece of work. About 5 o'clock this morning a large ship passed on our starboard but as our first mate had then the command of the vessel being his watch and in haste to crowd sail he did not run up our colours, and in consequence the other vessel did not hoist hers, which, when the captain came to understand he found fault with the mate saying he ought to have hoisted our flag being only common civility, so in this case neither ship could tell who each other was. At 9 o'clock thermometer at 68 on 4th day the same. I may notice here that our cargo consists of flour, ashes and cotton. We had also on board seventeen hundred and forty nine letters (besides counting house parcels) all of which I this day assisted the captain to assort and put into their proper bags - of course I had the opportunity of seeing the address of many houses that were known to me in England. In the evening a schooner passed astern at a great distance - so closed a fine and pleasant day.

7th day the 20th

A fine sun shining morning with sea almost as smooth as a mill pond, the wind rather ahead, the ship being close hauled yet just able to lay her course at the rate of about 6 knots an hour. Thermometer at 61, yesterday at 68. All sails set with fine and pleasant weather. Today one of our passengers met with a disappointment which I will here notice. Some of his friends previous to our leaving America had presented him with a bottle of sirup which he packed amongst his cloths in his box. When on examining for it this morning he found that the cork had worked out and the liquid run amongst his cloths - a most dirty set indeed - this suffices to shew the great impropriety of carrying bottles of anything in trunks amongst cloths whilst travelling. In the evening very clear and moon light, the wind at same time coming round more to the westward. So closed this day with easy sailing.

1st day the 21st

A fair westerly wind with a little rain. This morning in sight three vessels all on our starboard - a ship, Brig and schooner. About noon another small vessel hove into sight and at the dusk of the evening a large ship crossed very near to us - but as the west wind was then blowing fresh as also raining we did not speak each other. This was the fifth vessel we had in company today. We were favoured with fair westerly wind the whole of this day having our studing sails set from morning till night, so closed another sale both with wind and rain.

2nd day the 22nd

A fine cool pleasant morning. Thermometer 59 and again a head wind say from the north east. I may notice here that the length of our ship Amity's deck was 107 feet by 28 feet wide, the main mast from the deck 100 feet high, the miszen and foremast in proportion. Also ascertained the calculation of throwing the log line. If the 28 second sand glass be used then 15 yards 1 foot of line is a knot. If a 14 second glass then half the number of yards of log line. To shew the preciousness of fresh water at sea, the following instance may serve as a specimen - the cabin passengers are allowed fresh water to wash themselves, afterwards it is put into a bucket and the sailors have it in turns to wash their trousers and shirts in - at second hand being far preferable to salt water. In the afternoon rainy misty weather with a great swell of sea.

3rd day the 23rd

After a wild and wet night this morning rather more favourable, the ship going about 6 knots an hour in her direct course. Now cold raw weather thermometer in the shade on deck at 58. The sun today passes the line. In the afternoon the Equinox gale began to blow from the north west very fair for vessels steering east. Towards the evening our men lost the log and line; the ship being then running before the wind very fast so as to wind all the line of the reel, it not being properly fastened was all gone at once. The Captain was very severe with the mate for this trifling loss, though he could by no means help it - the wind now was very high with showers of rain. The sea also got into mountains.

4th day the 24th

After a sleepless night by most on board accompanied with a dreadful motion of rolling from side to side of pans, pots and every loose thing, together an aweful clatter, the daylight once more came on which seemed to relieve us a little. Wind and sea dreadful indeed. Our ship was stripped to bare poles saving a little fore sail and double leefed top sails, just enough to keep her before the wind with which she drifted or scudded eastwards from 10 to 12 knots an hour. Our deck was almost now continuously under water. We about 9 o'clock passed a Brig laying too and had we been bound to westward we must have undoubtedly have been in the same situation. At noon the captain and mate got the observation as accurately as they could and for our tossing night we had to console ourselves with the pleasure of having gone over 240 miles during the last 24 hours in our direct course homewards. In the evening and night still high sea and violent motion although some little moderated.

5th day the 25th

We were roused up this morning by our captain speaking with a British Brig, but as the vessel was running high the vessels could not bring very close too so that little could be understood what each other said, and accordingly our colours were hauled down again. We has besides the above Brig two other ships in sight near our starboard quarter and the other on the larboard bow. The weather this morning seemed to clear up a little, the wind from northwestand not so high as on the last two days and nights. The sun also shone very pleasantly. This was a great favour - none but those on sea are capable of judging or realising the change from a high rough wind and water to a mild day and smooth sea. At noon a good observation in lattitude 49-21 and longitude 16-00 soon after which the gale renewed its violence.

6th day the 26th

A very rough aweful night and still continuing. This forenoon we began to be very anxious as being aware of our fast approaching towards the Irish shores - with tremendous wind and sea behind us - the passengers offered the sailors a reward of five guineas for the first man to discover land. Thermometer in the shade on deck at 53. About 1 o'clock got an observation and sounding the first time found we were over a sandy bottom in about 80 to 100 fathoms of water, the wind at the same time blowing furiously. Now being at the mouth of the Irish Channel the Captain immediately laid the ship too. We had been driven by the gale in our direct course the last 24 hours 250 miles, a great distance in so short a time, just about three weeks since leaving Sandy Hook and losing sight of Long Island. At 5 o'clock the gale abated a little where upon the Captain put the ship again before the wind under easy sail. The wind and sea gradually becoming more gentle and calm. About eight o'clock I undressed and went to bed, not having had my cloths off for several days, being almost wore out for want of sleep, but tonight was favoured with 6 or 8 hours of good rest which refreshed me very much.

7th day the 27th

About 7 o'clock one of our company aroused us by exclaiming land in sight. We accordingly dressed and went on deck, when to our great satisfaction we had Cape Sale (or Kinsale) in view with a long range of hills all along the Irish coast as far as Cork. We were now favoured with a gentle breeze and smooth water, the hurricane having entirely subsided. We also had exchanged our bright blue water for the river colour. An Irish fishing boat soon found us and one of our company, an Irishman, hired it for two guineas to take him ashore so he had the opportunity of getting home before we could make Liverpool as the shore appeared not more than 8 or 10 miles from us. Our Captain exchanged a bottle of rum for some fresh fish with the fishermen and then ordered them to put off which they did and we also filled our sails and got on again. The weather now was become more serene and fine. The men turned too, as they call it, and handed up all our sails so that in a few hours we were from bare poles dressed out in grand order again having main royal and the other light canvas all out. The fishermen informed us that they had experienced dreadful weather for the last few days past. The forenoon being very fine with assistance of the glass we could see the Irish villages on shore and the corn and potatoe fields very clear, as also numbers of all sorts of vessels passing to and from Ireland. These were to us pleasing prospects after being tossed up and down the Atlantic ocean for about three weeks. At 4 o'clock passed abreast of the Dunganon Mountains and had a fair view of Waterford. The day was particularly fine and the wind in our favour nearly even on our stern. The men began to get the cables ready and the anchors over the bow. At about 6 o'clock passed the Saltees Islands say on our larboard and from that to nine o'clock sailed in sight of the Tuskan lighthouse. The wind being brisk the next place aimed at was the Holyhead light about 90 miles from our present situation, very moonlight and breeze favourable.

1st day the 28th

At 6 o'clock close in with Holyhead and soon afterwards passed the Skerries light and rocks, we had also in view on our left the range of Welch mountains. The sea was running rather high with a good deal of motion yet not particularly rough. Several vessels in sight around us, next passed near to the Isle of Anglesea, and at nine o'clock we took the pilot on board. Other two ships which we had passed this morning were astern of us and both had signals up for pilots. The boat after leaving us immediately proceeded to furnish the others with conductors into port. At half past nine o'clock off Great Ormshead - brisk wind and shining morning. About 12 o'clock came in sight of our native land the Cheshire hills now bore nearly ahead of us, as also the floating light and Liverpool light house, at half past one turned the Rock and we were now in the River Mersey.

At two dropped anchor opposite the pierhead, and about three o'clock we landed once more safe on our native shore after the short passage of twenty three days from leaving Sandy Hook and losing sight of America - for this very great favour and blessing may I never lose sight of the great bestower and protector both on land and sea. We then went to our old inn, the Star and Garter in Paradise Street, but they being quite full of company could not take us in, so we next went to the Liverpool Arms in Castle Street where after writing home and taking refreshment we were glad to retire to bed not having had any quiet rest for nearly two weeks.

2nd day the 29th

Our attention was now taken up with getting the luggage off the ship and passing the custom house with great diligence we compleated before the business closed - as the westerly winds had continued blowing for 8 or 10 days from 15 to 20 sail of vessels were got up this morning, all anxious to get into dock during todays high water, such confusion and clamour as I never before saw, people flocking to gase, with the ships crews, pilots and mates swearing and bawling out, was quite shocking. A large ship in her hurry run down a Welch sloop reducing her to a perfect wreck, and it was with great difficulty that they could get her into shoal water. JF having by this time got through which he proposed, we accordingly about 4 o'clock set out from Liverpool in the coach towards Manchester where we arrived at 9 o'clock in the evening and after seeing a few friends got to bed on still ground again.

3rd day 9th month the 30th

Left Manchester at seven in the morning and arrived at Longroyd Bridge about half past eleven where to my great satisfaction I found my dear wife, children and family all well, after being absent from them for six months, the gratitude and thankfulness of my hart on this occasion may be better conceived than described. The foregoing four small books of Memorandums I give to my wife, Mary Adamson and my children Emma Adamson, Edward Adamson and William Adamson for their use and perusal.

John Adamson

Longroyd Bridge

9th month 30th 1817

This drawing depicts a stagecoach of the type John Adamson would have travelled on between Huddersfield and Liverpool. The Cornwallis coach ran from 1812 to 1839 between Leeds and Manchester via Huddersfield, the journey taking some seven and a half hours. The cost of this journey in 1813 was 12/- inside the coach or 8/- outside.

NEW YORK
PHILADELPHIA
BOSTON
ALBANY
HARTFORD
BALTIMORE
WILMINGTON
NEW HAVEN
NEW LONDON
NEW BEDFORD
TAUNTON
NORTHAMPTON
LEBANON
SALEM
MILFORD
DELAWARE
NEW BERLIN
LONG ISLAND
Long Island Sound
ATLANTIC
OCEAN
Atlantic City
Longitude West of Greenwich
76°
74°
72°
B
C
D
E

Ackworth School, 12th Mo. 20th 1830

Dear Parents,
　　　　　Thinking it would be agreeable to you to receive a few lines from Ackworth, I embrace the opportunity of writing to you, to inform you, that I am in good health; and I hope this letter will find you and all the family well. Please to be so kind as to tell Benjamin Seebohm, that I am very much obliged to him for the books which he sent me. I should be very much obliged to you, if you would send me a clothes-brush. As Father requested me to send you word what trade I should prefer, that of a Joiner & Cabinet-maker is what I most incline to. A few weeks back, there was a wonderful calf brought to Ackworth from Pontifract, which had two heads and six legs, with other peculiarities. The weather here has, within this last week, been uncommonly wet. I have now begun to learn Geography. I am in the first class in Reading, and in the Second classes in Spelling, Grammar and Tables. We have had a few slides lately. The Committee has thought proper that the boys and girls should have plates instead of trenchers to eat their meals from. I should be very much obliged, if you would send me a "Natural History", and a little book entitled 'the Stolen boy'. Having nothing more to express at present, I conclude with dear love to you all. From

　　　　　　Your affectionate Son,
　　　　　　　　John Adamson.

A letter to John Adamson written in 1830 by his son John who attended Ackworth School

The District Registry of Wakefield.

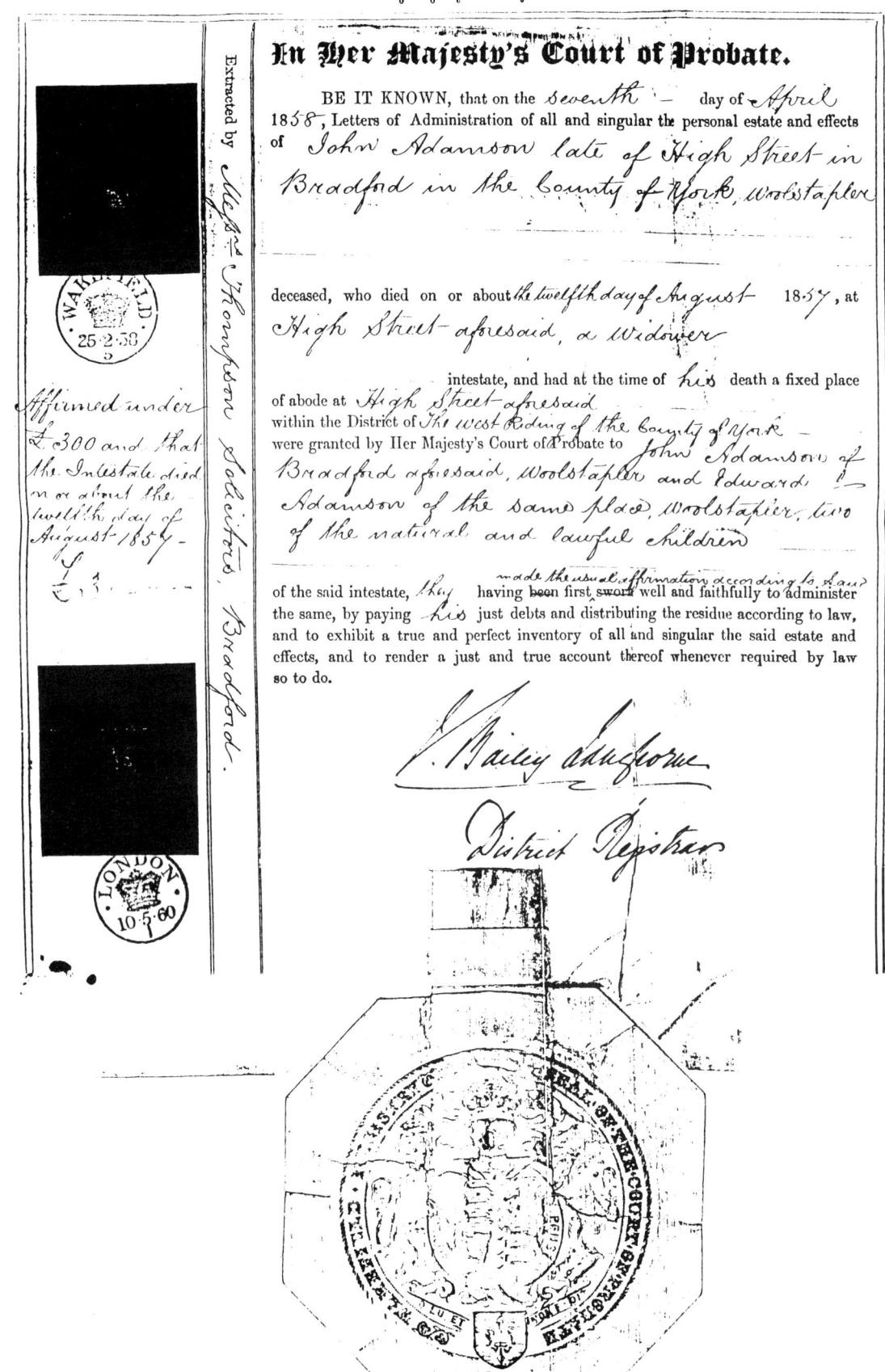

In Her Majesty's Court of Probate.

BE IT KNOWN, that on the seventh day of April 1858, Letters of Administration of all and singular the personal estate and effects of John Adamson late of High Street in Bradford in the County of York, Woolstapler

deceased, who died on or about the twelfth day of August 1857, at High Street aforesaid, a widower intestate, and had at the time of his death a fixed place of abode at High Street aforesaid within the District of the West Riding of the County of York were granted by Her Majesty's Court of Probate to John Adamson of Bradford aforesaid, Woolstapler and Edward Adamson of the same place, Woolstapler, two of the natural and lawful children of the said intestate, they made the usual affirmation according to Law having been first sworn well and faithfully to administer the same, by paying his just debts and distributing the residue according to law, and to exhibit a true and perfect inventory of all and singular the said estate and effects, and to render a just and true account thereof whenever required by law so to do.

T. Bailey Anglesore
District Registrar

Extracted by Messrs Thompson Solicitors Bradford.

Affirmed under £300 and that the Intestate died on or about the twelfth day of August 1857

It is believed that John Adamson was one of the first exporters of woollen cloth from Yorkshire, England to Germany. Below is reproduced a letter, written on parchment, from the Skipper of a ship at Whitby to John Adamson relating to a consignment of cloth which was ready for transportation from Whitby to Hamburg. Although the letter is undated, it is believed to have been written at some time between 1812 and 1816.

NOVEMBER THE 18 — SOR — WHE HARE AT WHITBY YET AND THINK WHE NEVER SHAL BE ABLE TO MAKE THE VOYAGE FOR THE WEATHER HES SO HORKED FOR SEVERAL MEN THAT HES VOUST TO COST THINKS BEST TO GET A NOTHER FESSEL TO PRECED THE VOYAGE WHCH I SUD WESH TO HEAR FROM YOU FOST WHAT YOU THINK BEST TO BE DUN FOR SHE HES DEEP WHICH WHE HAD GOT REDY TO SALE IUST BE FORE THE GALE CAME HON WHICH ONE OF THE PILETS SED TO ME WHICH HE SAID THAT WHOD BE A CHANGE OF WIND AND BY THAT WHE STOPE IF WE HAD BEN AT SEA HIT WHOD BEEN GOD HELP HUS FOR THE GALE WOS MOR LIKE THUNDER THEN WIND WITH HUS FOR THERE HES 8 HOR 9 SHIPS LOST A BOUT COSTS OF WHITBY WICH I RIT TO MARCHAT TO LET EM NOW THAT WHE WHOD HAT WHITBY BUT GOT NO HANSER FROM HIM WICH IF YOU THINK BEST TO LIVER OR NOT WICH THINK IT WHIL FOR THIS GALE HES MAD THE MAN GO HOME THAT I HAD BY THE MONTH AND IF ANE BODY COM FOR ANE MONEY NOT TO GEV NONE FOR HE LEFT BY HIS OWN COUNT AND I HAVE NO MAN AT PRESENT WICH I SHOULD WISH TO HEAR FROM YOU WHETHER YOU WOULD HAVE HOR TO LIVER OR NOT FOR 2 MEN WILL BE VERRY DEAR FOR I SHAL BE FAST FOR MONEY SOWN WICH IF CONSIDER TO BE LIVERD HAT WHITBY I WOULD HAVE YOU TO RIGHT IF YOU PLES TO THE MARCHAT WICH IS NAME M JOSEPH TOWCE GRANGEMOUTH FOR NO MEN CARS TO GO WITH ME FOR THEY THINK SHE IS NOT ABLE TO GET HOR PASSAG THIS WINTER TIME WICH I WESH WE WOS SAFE LIVERD AND AT HOME FOR I HAM HUNEASEY BEN SO LONG WICH I HOPE YOU WILL LET ME HEAR FROM YOU M FOSTER AND NO MORE AT THIS TIME — ROBERT GIBSON

The letter reproduced below was a testament written by John Adamson to his wife, Mary, following her death in 1852. It would appear that the addition in the left margin was written at a later date by one of John's family as it reads 'She is now laid with father in Undercliffe'.

Memorandum by way of Testimony concerning my late dear Wife Mary Adamson, who departed this Life on the ninth day of third Month and was interred in Friends burial ground at Bradford the fourteenth of the same 1852 Aged near Seventy four Years and my Wife about Forty three Years.

I can in sincerity testify of the above dear deceased, that she was a highly respectable orderly and innocent Woman, A good industrious managing Wife, a tender Mother and kindly and friendly disposed towards all. Hence may we not humbly believe and trust that through the merits and mercies of an ever blessed and atoning Redeemer that she is permitted to join the happy of all Ages in praising and glorifying her God and Saviour for ever, Amen saith my Soul.

[left margin: She is now laid with father at Undercliffe]

Bradford
4 mo 29 1852

John Adamson

ADAMSON FAMILY TREE (CONDENSED)

Thomas Adamson (Thirsk, North Yorkshire)
died 1728

Mary
died 9.11.1742

3 children including John (Thirsk - Weaver)   born 19.10.1711
                                                     died 1751

married Elizabeth Dale   born 1709
                                                     died 20.1.1793

4 children including William (Husbandman)   born 4.11.1746
                                                     died 29.4.1806

married (i) Rebekah Hick   died 2.10.1789
                                    married (ii) Margaret - 3 children

6 children including John * (Wool Stapler)   born 14.3.1784
                                                     died 13.8.1857

married 15.6.1809 Mary Beaumont   born 31.7.1778
                                                     died 9.3.1852

4 children including John (Wool Merchant)   born 2.7.1818
                                                     died 18.3.1876

married 16.11.1852 Esdres Oates   born 1833
                                                     died 18.2.1919

7 children including Joseph   born 21.6.1861
                                                     died ?

married (i) Maria   born 1863
                                                     died 1892
                                    married (ii) Emma Jane Holt

4 children including Norman (Grocer)   born 24.11.1890
                                                     died 6.12.1973

married Mary Alexander   born 30.5.1884
                                                     died 2.10.1966

3 children including Kenneth #   born 18.9.1924

married (i) Mary Taylor   born 28.12.1921
                                                     died 12.3.1976
                                    married (ii) Pat Buckley

    * Our diarist
    # The present custodian of the diaries.

Kenneth Adamson appears to be the last of the Adamson line.

ACKNOWLEDGEMENTS

During the additional research carried out in connection with the publication of John Adamson's diaries, help has been freely given by a host of people and organisations (listed below) on both sides of the Atlantic to each of whom I extend my sincere thanks.

Albany Institute of History and Art, USA

Lt.Cdr. J.W.Beck R.N., Falmouth Maritime Museum

Bradford Industrial Museum

Bradford Libraries

Brotherton Library, Leeds - Special Collections Department

Commission for Racial Equality, London

F.Davies, Ackworth Quaker School

Leeds Leisure Services

Liverpool Maritime Museum

Russell Mortimer, Leeds

The Mayor of New York, USA

The Mayor of Philadelphia, USA

National Maritime Museum, Greenwich

National Museum of Science and Industry, London

New York Historical Society, USA

Peabody Museum of Salem, USA

Pennsylvania Academy of Fine Arts, USA

Philadelphia Historical Commission, USA

Quaker Library, Euston, London

Quaker Meeting Houses at Rawdon, nr.Leeds; Wooldale and Paddock nr.Huddersfield

Tate Gallery, London

Tolson Museum, Huddersfield.

In addition to those listed above, I extend my grateful thanks to the many individuals, too numerous to mention, who have helped me with this project

Valda A. Swain

Idle, Bradford   September 1992